To: T... Bdae Cobb Ah...
Hali

MW01515597

Thank you so much for your
Support and kind words. I am
happy that I met you all. Remember
Nothing is Impossible when God is on
your side! 😊

Said I Wouldn't

Tell It ....

But I Just Can't

Keep It To Myself

Nov. 26, 2023

Published by:
Christians Soulseeking Book Publishing
Jackson, Tennessee
tamekahicks360@gmail.com

SAID I WOULDN'T TELL IT ....

BUT I JUST CAN'T KEEP IT TO MYSELF

Tameka Hicks

Christians Soulseeking
Book Publishing
Jackson, Tennessee

Table of Contents

Dedication

I would first like to dedicate this book to God. This was truly a faith walk for me. None of this would have been possible without the anointing and hand of God so strongly on my life. I dare not forget to give Him the Glory and Honor because without Him I am truly nothing. It wasn't an easy walk but the relationship I built with Him is irreplaceable. Every move I made regarding this book was by the direction of God and his spoken Word. I promise there were moments I wanted to give up, but God kept showing me grace, mercy, and new strength to carry on. When I was at my last, and thought everything was over, God kept opening up a window and pouring out blessings I didn't have room enough to receive. I am a living testimony that the promises of God will not return void. He didn't fail me and I promise, if He gives you a vision, and you say yes, your life will never be the same. Thank you, God for trusting me and being patient with me.

I also dedicate this book to my middle school and high school principal, Mrs. Janice Epperson. You never gave up on me. You pushed me every day to be the best I could be. You always taught me to take care of business. It's true that parents are not the only ones that raise you, but it takes a team effort. Thank you for believing in me and having so much faith in me when I didn't have any in myself. I will always remember you. You touched my life every day. May God bless you and forever keep you. You had a passion to teach your students and push us to be all God called us to be. Thank you for every lesson you taught me for the direction you gave me.

Lastly, I want to dedicate this to my mother and godparents. It took all three of you to raise me. You are all wise and strong people. Your teaching was not in vain. It hasn't always been easy for any of us, but we always held on to God and pulled through. Thank you for taking time out of your life to train me in the way I should go and for loving me. Thank you, Mom, for adopting me and sacrificing so much so that I could have a better life. Thank you Godmother and Godfather for stepping in and taking a little stress off my mom and taking care of me.

Acknowledgments

I would like to take this opportunity to thank all who encouraged me to continue this journey with God. Your kind actions and comments were right on time, and I am grateful. I would like to thank my college, Xavier University, for sticking with me and by me during one of my darkest times. Your support and dedication was not overlooked.

To my professors, thank you for constantly encouraging me to stay in the race and to never give up.

To all my family, friends, mentors, and spiritual mothers and fathers, thank you from the bottom of my heart for constantly supporting me, challenging me, and encouraging me to do great things. I needed every word you spoke into my heart and spirit.

To my church home, Greater St. Luke Baptist Church, in Jackson Tennessee, Pastor Marvin and First Lady Hall, thank you for always being there when I needed you the most and giving me the opportunity to share and express the gift God instilled into me. I am forever grateful.

I want to give a special shout out of thank you to my godparents, Stanley Fields and Geraldine Kingfield, and my mother Brenda Hicks for raising me since the age of three to be a God-fearing lady of God. I learned so many lessons from you.

I want to give a special shout out to Mrs. Kristin, thank you for allowing God to use you. You were like my mother away from home. No matter what, you made sure I was doing well and well-taken care of. Thanks for opening up your home and warming arms to me down in New Orleans.

To Mr. Hal Clark and Wyldfm family, thank you for allowing me to interview on such a large and respected platform, which was the Sunday Journal. That blessed me more than words can say.

To Mrs. Cynthia Mann, you are my heart. Thank you for always stepping in and helping my mother and me when we were struggling. You have been such a huge blessing to my life and nothing you have said or done for me has gone unnoticed. I am truly grateful!

Lastly, thank you to Good News Talk CEO, Mrs. Connie Alsobrook. You gave me a wonderful interview and article from the start. God bless you.

If I missed anyone, because there are so many I could thank that touched and changed my life, please charge it to my head not my heart. It truly took everyone that crossed my path for me to be the person I am today. Thank you. Thank you.

Thank you God, You are so good to me!

This powerful and intriguing piece announces God's victory over evil. This is God at His best. Tameka's fascinating story captures it well. Only God can claim the baggage of our own lives.

– Fr. Etido Jerome, SSJ, University Chaplain
Xavier University of Louisiana

Personal Reflection

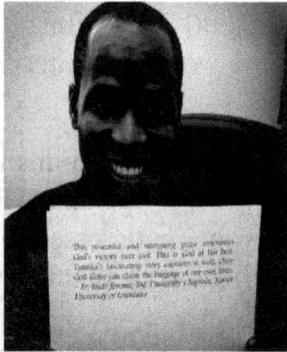

Tameka's compelling personal experience of God's victory of evil walks us into the mystery of God. This message offers the simple hope that the messiness of our lives is not beyond repair. It announces God as the fixer of all things.

I find this piece appropriate for all people. Also, it has in it the power to inspire all who acknowledge the power of God to break every chain through Christ. Tameka, I agree with you that only God alone can claim the baggage of our lives. God does not only claim them, He destroys them through the power of His love on the cross. I hope this inspires many to pursue the way of love, peace, and joy.

-Fr. Etido Jerome SSJ, University Chaplain
Xavier University of Louisiana

Introduction

I know God didn't call me to quit and give up whenever things got rough in my life. He called me to stand as a witness for Him. He had to strip me down so I could see the distractions that were placed in my path. I had to see that I was going in the wrong direction and I had to be turned around. This time – and this was something new - God ordered me the assignment that I feared at such a young age. I denied who I was to let God use me for His will and His way. I began to thirst like never before for more and more of His word. I began to stop caring what people thought of me, and the hurt I had once experienced became the hurt I started to embrace. I can't tell you how happy and passionate I am about God and His word. I am just like you: imperfect and in need of His words.

I found myself crying tears of joy instead of tears of sorrow. I found myself praying for strength and confirmation as well as direction. I am not a saint, but I am truly a child of the almighty King. I chose to weave poetry, scriptural references, and direct messages from God through my life into a book that will bless mightily. Through this, the mess of the world was made cleaner - less murky, less confused, less chaotic. I pray you are blessed beyond measure, for this book is not written to expose my life, but to unveil the greater message that God spoke in and through me.

Every day there is someone that is crying for that word that will speak to not just their emotions, but their life and spirit. There are a lot of reasons for this, but I believe the primary reason is that many mothers and fathers are losing themselves, and their sons and daughters, because of influences of a society in decline. How many young women does it take being diagnosed with HIV, before us, as people, understand that sex is not the answer? How many men does it take to be buried at such a young age, killed by gunshot wounds, before we truly understand that violence is a corruption of the solution? How many mothers do we have to hear cry out before we realize that abuse is not acceptable, whether it be mental, physical, or sexual? How many corners and prison cells do we have to visit to understand that no matter who is president, nothing will change unless we as witnesses take a stand?

The Bible says "We will reap what we sow" (Galatians 6:9). Nothing could be clearer to humankind in our times. There are things in the making, and things already happening, stemming from of the sin of mankind. God is getting ready to unleash something upon the Earth that will be in full effect very soon. Despite the rejection of God by a lot of the world, there is a need for Christians to live holy so that those not blessed by His light might see our example. The devil is getting ready to prey on us and on our traditional paths and ways. The things that we used to do in the past to get by will no longer work (such as only claiming God when it is convenient for our lifestyles). We can win the righteous battle only by trusting in and obeying the Word of God.

We have been so scared of change. We crawl in our shells and feel everything is all right as is. The worst thing we can do right now in our lives is give in to the enemy's power and fame. That power has generated a world of confusion. It's not about what we don't know right now, it's about what God is trying to let us know. It's about His Word that we have ignored over and over again, because we were afraid to truly stand for Him.

As Christians, we have been placed as misfits on this earth and we have given up on the authority we have in our lives. We all are misfits in some shape, form, or fashion. We all feel some days like we just don't mix with the world. However, we aren't supposed to mix. God created us all differently and there was a reason behind it. God has a different calling and purpose on all our lives. The answer is not money nor politics. The answer to restoring and recovering the life we can live is walking in faith, being totally committed to God's will and word.

We are missing the bigger picture of the mess that is going on in the world right now. God is trying to get our attention in every form possible. Yet we are so blinded by what our fleshly eyes can see, ignorant to what our spiritual eyes are trying to reveal to us, we become detached and distracted by Satan's work. We have taken our eyes off God - I believe God is sending these messages forth, not so we can read them and throw them back on the shelf without change, but so we can conclude how real God is and how much we must put every inch of faith in him. This shifts everything we might want in life. It's no longer acceptable to judge the next person because he or she doesn't resemble our character or physical features. We can't judge the things we used to do in the same light. Our lives without God tell us nothing about who we are. We are too focused on ourselves and that is the very reason order cannot be restored. God is not pleased. There is coming a time when we will be asked to deny Christ and His Word.

There is going to be a time when the Bible will not exist. God is trying to relay the warning signs of the truth to our daughters, sons, mothers, and fathers before the Day of Judgment and the Antichrist reveals itself. At this time, we will no longer be allowed to pray to God, cry out to Him or study and read His word, the weapon that will save us in spiritual warfare. Nevertheless, we serve a mighty God and Lucifer will have to abandon his destructive plans for our lives, because he too cannot deny the Word of God. The enemy knows once God speaks, everyone must open his or her heart and listen.

God is the reason that my soul rejoices and the devil no longer can fight me the way he used to. I ask you right now - are you ready for the truth? Are you ready to deny yourself and your will before Satan destroys you? Do you want to restore your life to what God desires for it to be, and get the confirmation you've been seeking to fulfill your purpose? The world can't change if the ones that refer to themselves as Christians keep backing down in fear and choose not to stand boldly for God. The Word of God is our weapon. It's time now to read it and plant it deep in our soul before we no longer have access to it.

I thank you in advance for your support. I am praying that you will be renewed, restored, and transformed by my story and the messages God has revealed to me to help me through my storm. I am a living testimony that God is real, and He is ready for you to experience a breakthrough like you've never seen.

Before you begin reading this book, ask God for understanding to hear exactly what he is trying to get across to you. I believe that everything happens for a reason. It is no mistake that the words God has given me are being delivered and you are getting ready to walk a journey of faith. I strongly believe that these powerful words will not only change your life mentally, but spiritually as well.

As you read this book, I want you to think about your life and the confusion that you have encountered or are facing right now. I ask you to seek God in every word that you hear and read, because the enemy doesn't desire for you to hear anything God says. It is up to us to not only hear the Word that God speaks, but position ourselves to be obedient and apply that Word to our lives. It doesn't matter who you are or how many times you have sinned. If you are ready to be informed, encouraged, and set free then it is time to flip to the next page. God bless you and forever keep you.

Prayer of Faith

Dear God,
I ask you right now for understanding
I ask you right now to remove
all distractions and clear my mind
I thank you in advance for the things in my life
that are about to take place
I know I am a sinner and I am not worthy
of your grace and mercy
Please forgive me for walking
the wrong path over and over again
Speak to my heart and soul, for I need a word
that will heal and restore me
I confess that my life is a mess right now
and I want you to lead my path
Let me deny my own beliefs and ways,
and clearly see that I need to adapt to yours
I ask you for confirmation and direction
Let me see my own faults and not the faults
of my brothers and sisters
I know you are real and sometimes I deny that fact
I am choosing to trust and lean on your word
and promises for my life
I am a misfit in this world,
but I know that comes with a relationship with you
Minister to my hurt and pain,
and let your presence enter in

One last thing, God—
Thank you for every blessing you have given me
in the past and will give me in the future.
I claim it in the name of your Son, Jesus. Amen.

Chapter 1

Does God Hate Me?

Does God Hate me? This is the question, I constantly heard throughout my journey and talking to different people around the world. Many have lost hope. I have the gift to help people see God's forgiveness, grace, and love through faith. I have been walking with Christ since I was seven years old. I have never seen the wrath of God or ever felt it in my life. I have experienced hurt from people. However, through the gift of the Holy Spirit, when I see people I don't see their faults, I see their heart. Sometimes I feel people can use religion as a means of power to control and manipulate people rather than help them grow, prosper, and live successful. What I'm seeing and running into is a lot of our generation and some older people are turning away from God or not believing in Him because he is presented in such a mean and cruel way by people who say they love God.

Maybe I'm wrong in my approach to my stance or approach to this subject, but how can we lead people to Christ, tell them He died for their sins, and in the same tongue condemn them to hell.

God is compassionate and understanding. Ministry is about

being transparent and humble. Every day we fall short in some way to the rules and ways of God. How do we expect people who are just coming to know God to walk so holy and upright? Shouldn't our main objective be that they walk with God and grow a relationship with him? People are hiding their face from a God that sees them so differently than we as people do. Aren't we the ones that will have to answer to why so many never felt the love and embrace of God? Aren't we going to be judged in the same manner that we judge others? God doesn't love us with conditions. If that's the case, we all would have missed heaven. God finds us to love on us, show us who we really are, and break us from guilt and shame.

Back in the day people were forced into religion and God never intended that. He wanted us to worship and love him freely. Sometimes I wonder if it is our assignment to help change someone's behavior or just give them the God that saved us and let Him do the rest. God *is* in control, right? So should we live with the worry about our loved ones in the place they are right now? Can we really change that? I think what makes everyone unique is their story, their journey, their own walk with Christ.

If we, as Christians, prematurely step in and try to stop the process, how can someone truly understand the unconditional love that God has for them? How can their faith grow or be tested? How can the word be not just preached or read but lived and applied?

As I'm reading the four gospels, Christ won people through helping them, healing them, teaching them, understanding them, and allowing them to grow. I don't see anywhere where he stopped or rejected anyone. He purposely picked followers who were messed up and imperfect. God shows us grace and the gift of mercy.

What if God found me and the first thing he did was to point out my sins and tell me I'm going to hell? Would I truly be who I am right now? If God is love he can't be hate, right? Are we, as followers, putting more weight and pressure on ourselves than what God intended?

If God says he will never leave nor forsake us and he came that we might have life and have it more abundantly and that we were made fearfully and wonderfully, why do we find ourselves hiding from Him, handing out masks with good intentions, but drowning in tears of self-sabotage years down the road?

Isn't our number one calling to know Christ and accept Him as our Savior? We will have trouble, losses, setbacks, misunderstandings, doubt, heartbreaks, worry, anxiety. But God doesn't change his mind about us, regardless. He doesn't count our wrongs. He doesn't speak down on us.

He gifted you, chose you, and gave you a vision no eye can see. Don't keep asking why me God. Stop feeling unworthy. Dare to believe God in the midst of your insecurities, in the midst of your own pain. Sometimes the blessing is in your weakness and hidden under His Almighty power and strength.

The first step is admitting you are young, you are not that wise, you are not that strong, and you can't bear the weight of this world on your own. We are not waiting on God, God is waiting on us. Dare to walk on water with him. Dare to believe Him to do something through you that naturally may seem impossible. If we are all created differently but God abides in us doesn't that mean our journeys will never be the same? The only thing I believe we all have in common is believing in something greater then what we are in this time frame. Ultimately, unimaginable faith. Faith was never meant to divide and separate. It was meant to empower and enlighten. Light and darkness cannot go together.

Chapter 2

This is My Season

Many times in life when we describe the word "season," we think about the weather. It can be winter, fall, spring or summer. We don't always know or understand why seasons were made, but we all know that they are designed for a purpose. What comes to mind when you think of winter? Maybe you see extreme weather, so much darkness in the way, and you just want to stay inside and hide yourself from everything. Others might see falling snow and richer times at home. I want you to think for a second and ask yourself what makes your favorite season great?

No matter what season you see as your favorite, it is going to have some good and bad days. We can decide which season we like the most, but we have no control over when it is our season of purpose to be filled or revealed by Him. "There is an appointed time for everything. And there is a time for every event under heaven. A time to give birth and a time to die; a time to plant and a time to uproot what is planted" (Ecclesiastes 3:1). We often try to predict what age we will die, how much pain we can endure, or how long the ones that we love the most see us as valuable and important. Think for a second - when was the last time you sat and worried about what others thought about you or how many times the devil has knocked you down? Whether we want to admit it or not, we give the devil more of the glory in our lives than God Himself.

The question I deal with the most (and answer) is *how do you know God's voice?* I learned during my spiritual wilderness and many complications of life that God will speak straight to your heart right before it reaches your mind. We have to be able to position ourselves to be a vessel for God, not to make sure everything in our life is perfect. We aren't meant to be our own God - we need to learn to embrace everything that God allows to take place in our lives.

I had to realize the difference between season and moment. A *moment of time* is not the same as a *season in time.* I wish I could go back in time and change the bad moments and encounters that took place in my life, but I will never regret the seasons in my life. "For his anger lasts only a moment, but his favor lasts a lifetime; weeping may stay for the night, but rejoicing comes in the morning" (Psalm 30:5). Once examining this particular scripture, I realized that though we may feel anxiety, pain, frustration, and heartache for a moment in time, God's season of purpose is the key to renewing all we thought we lost in those moments. The seasons that took place caused me pain, hurt, and a lot of tears, but they didn't kill or break me. My pain actually restored me from myself at times. As a child, I thought as a child would and did childish things to get through life. I thank God that now I can see the error of my ways, and I was renewed and restored enough to realize that my way was never the best way.

My ways caused me to be in a state of confusion, not knowing who to trust, when to trust, or even how to trust. It caused me to hide myself and who I was to please society. It was not easy waking up at night feeling like I was constantly falling into my own pit of hell. I went to sleep at times, hoping that God would take me out and let me stay asleep because I was miserable. I had no peace, no joy, no understanding of God or life. I was just going through the motions and the routine of what I thought a Christian should be and act like. I would go to school and class wearing a smile, all while I had thoughts of killing myself in the back of my head. At times, in class, I would lose myself and drift into a state of depression. I felt like I was closer and closer to having a breakdown while the weight of the world was getting heavier and heavier.

I was so confused about my identity, my heart, my emotions, and even, at times, myself. I began to be disgusted with life. I couldn't stand walking past a mirror or anything that reminded me of my own reflection. I couldn't understand why I could hear the words "I love you" over and over again, but never feel love. I didn't understand why people that I cared for so much only got close to me to hurt me and see me spiral down. I couldn't understand why God allowed me to even cross paths with people that He knew meant me only harm.

The reason God allows for storms in our lives is not so that we lose ourselves in the storm, but so that we connect and find Him while passing through it. If it had not been for the storms and the imperfections I was given to deal with, I would have been too comfortable in life to allow God to move me. When we get comfortable with something or someone we will never be disgusted by anything they say or do – this includes ourselves. We will allow even what we don't feel is morally right to take place right in front of our eyes.

As God spoke to me on the night of our encounter in my dorm room at Xavier University, he told me that it was time to stop hiding and running away from my problems. He said to me, *I placed everyone in your path for a specific reason and purpose and now it is time for you to understand why.*

Have you ever reached a place in life where you just felt alone? Where regardless of who reaches out to you, you reject them all? I was at that place in my life. I didn't care about anything or anyone anymore. I was existing on this earth but I had stopped living. I was so overtaken that I went to sleep with nightmares and woke up to even greater nightmares, which played like a permanent movie. So many things triggered the pain.

No matter how much I was giving up on God, He never began to give up on me. One night He came to me in a loud voice. I didn't know what to do so I tried to ignore it and continue with what I was doing (having a pity party). The voice grew louder and louder, as if God knew I wouldn't listen unless I knew without a doubt it was Him. He told me that what I had experienced was not in vain. He told me that my life, though I felt it was useless, was just right for His purpose. I couldn't help it, but I was frightened because I thought God was angry with me. I told God that I was too young, unclean, misused, and broken to have any type of calling or purpose on my life. In my encounter with God He reminded me of who I really was, not what my experiences had defined me to be. He told me I wasn't a mistake and I wouldn't inherit any more devilish traits, but only if I started to follow Him and not my own way in life.

He let me know that I wasn't ugly, inside or out, but I was beautifully and wonderfully made in His image. He let me know that though I didn't have any contact with my biological parents, that it didn't mean I wasn't a child of His. He spoke life into me at the moment when I was about to give up on myself, my education, and everyone else. He let me know that I was a fighter and it wasn't in me to quit, no matter how much I wanted to.

I never knew this but I learned that fear was faith in Satan. Real faith is trusting and understanding God's power. For so long I had been speaking negatively about my life, emphasizing everything I could not do, forgetting to honor and glorify God for everything He had already put me through. In this encounter with God, He let me know that my past could no longer hold me back. I was so dependent on my own strength that I neglected the strength of God that was in me.

I had been convinced so long that my future was in the hands of the enemy, but I failed to see that God was the hand that was covering me every time I rested and opened my eyes. He said, *Every heartache you bear, will be gone in my name. My anointing is about to be released within you. I need you to stop running from me and trying to hide from my will. If you put me first again, and grab hold to my unconditional love, I will heal you, restore you, and renew your mind. It's time to stop depending and leaning on your own strength. It's time to stop trying to bear the weight of the world alone. Just freely give your life over to me.* As God spoke to my heart, it was as if He was sitting right next to me with His arms wrapped around me, letting me know how much He truly loved me.

I supernaturally reached a state of peace like never before. My encounter with God was a life-changing experience. I have always heard that you will not be the same once you enter the presence of God, but I never believed it until that moment. The tears that once flooded my pillow because of sorrow now started to flood my hands because of joy, a joy I had never experienced in my life. I had known God all my life and heard about Him, but I never imagined He would speak directly to me and that I would feel so free afterwards.

One thing I will never forget is when God told me that He gave me a big heart for a reason. I was going about life thinking that loving intensely was a curse, but God didn't desire for it to be a curse, but rather a blessing that brings about passion, understanding, and love for all people. He revealed to me that I had a promise to fulfill and Satan wanted to trick me into giving that all up. He said, *The devil knows your purpose before I even reveal it to you, because I allow him to break you, therefore you can seek me and I can restore, and build you again. I am tired of you trying to halfway love me but love everyone else as if they are your God.* He said, *The devil wants to take you out because I am about to give you a task, that I can only trust you with. Do not worry about your past, or your future. It is time to focus on your season that's overdue.* He told me that he called me to a place right now of victory, not defeat, and that I had to believe that for myself. God told me that He didn't call me to a place of anger, despair, hurt, or tears, but a place of strength that I never thought I had. He gave me, in that moment, a spirit of boldness and humbleness.

There was one question I had to ask - Why me, God?

He said, *You are witness to my miracles and power within ... think about your life and how many times you were in dangerous situations and my hands covered you so that you would be untouched. I know you are young and you don't want this responsibility, but if you keep following my path and directions, I will bless you with favor and increase in the end. You are weak right now. You are confused and you feel too broken to be used by me. However, that is exactly why I desire to have you as my vessel.*

God reminded me of how many times he knocks on broken and confused souls like mine who reject Him and what He tries to do in our lives.

He asked me for one favor - to let my story no longer glorify the devil, which many my age tend to do, but glorify Him instead. He did not want me to let the hurtful experiences, the bruises, and my broken heart to draw me away from Him. He wanted me to draw many others nearer to His love. I was in awe, because I didn't understand my gift just yet. God told me that His anointing would carry me through the process, and when I felt I couldn't handle it, He would step right in, on time, to help me along. He said, *I am getting ready to send you through your own wilderness. It is going to feel like I am not there because now that you know your calling and my voice, I need you to pass the test before I allow you to be able to reach millions around the world.*

He made me understand that I wasn't prepared yet to receive what He had for me, but if I stayed in His will, His Word wouldn't return to me empty. He said, *As you go through this wilderness, I'll appear in this same voice. I'll give you the chapters you need for the book I want you to write. I will give you every resource to make it happen as long as you continue to give me the glory.*

All of a sudden the voice was gone, and I fell straight to my knees. I started to worship God like never before. I called out his name like never before. With this, He stayed faithful to His word and promises. Now I am able to boldly declare that if it wasn't for God, I would be nothing. I want you to understand that this book is not about religions acts or values. It's about the relationship and commitment to God that we must all have and that we all need to get through life. God desires for us to love Him with our whole heart, not because we are obligated to, but because we truly have fallen in love with Him.

I want you to know that everything I went through was in divine order. It had to happen to get these messages into your hands. I want you to understand that whatever you are going through right now, there is purpose in it. God doesn't waste trials. He will not give you more than He feels you can bear. I encourage you to step out of your own way. Release everything that has you bound or distracted from where God wants to take you. God does not want us to be miserable and stuck in self-loathing. He wants us to know that when our season is due, nothing in hell can stop His will.

I thought my sexual assault experience was the end for me, but it was actually the beginning of my life. I thought a broken heart was the end of love, but God meant for it to be the beginning of His real love. Giving up is never an option. God will always see you through, but only if you believe in Him without doubt. I encourage you to look back over your life and thank God for His love and the reach of His hands over your life. Without God, we do not know where we are.

I am living proof that God is able and faithful because this is not the first time I thought the end was near (nor will it be the last). I know the God I serve will deliver me again.

We must not look at everything in a negative light, which causes us more stress, but in a bright light with a positive outlook on the pain we face and the headaches we sometimes must bear in life. I learned that healing is not overnight, but it can be done in full as a process of true deliverance.

This is your season to take back what the devil stole from you, even your peace of mind. Do not allow anyone to steal your joy. Though it hurts for the moment, God allows it, and there is truly purpose in your pain.

Chapter 3

There is Purpose in My Pain

Confirmation is the perfection of baptism, as performed in the Catholic faith. It is one of the Sacraments, and is usually received as a teenager several years after making one's First Communion. Confirmation is regarded as the perfection of Baptism because as the introduction to the Rite of Confirmation states, "the baptized are more perfectly bound to the church and are enriched with a special strength of the Holy Spirit." Hence, they are true witnesses of Christ, more strictly obliged to spread and defend the faith by word and deed. This is a moment that defines a Catholic as a servant of Christ and affirms meaning in one's life.

I had begun to give up on any type of purpose or calling that was on my life. At the moment, the mindset I had was negative. I felt my life had no meaning. Have you ever gotten to a place where you felt like your life was meaningless and your purpose was only to live and die? That's the story you woke up to every day? You worship the act of routine and even comfortable states? Well, that was me.

There was a time in my life when I felt completely alone and lost in the world, like no one cared about me. You see, at birth I was given up by my birth parents. I don't know them personally, however, it doesn't make me bitter or angry that they aren't in my life because I believe God had a bigger plan for my life. However, I didn't always feel that way -after being placed from foster home to foster home. My trust level bottomed out. I was abused mentally, emotionally, and physically. I can remember it like it was yesterday – starving, and not knowing if my foster mom was going to finally end my life. This was a woman that was placed as my parental guardian. She was not a loving and nurturing woman, rather the opposite. She was abusive physically as well as mentally. My foster mother gave the real mothers that took in orphans a bad name. She didn't ever tell me she loved me or that she wanted to see me succeed. She was not the type that cooked a warm dinner and fed me when I was hungry. I honestly felt that she hated me more than anything in the world. I lived in fear of the next strike to my back and face.

I learned quickly how to live on scrap food from the trash, because that is what I was fed countless times. She would leave me for days on end where there was nothing I could do but cry. I cried so much that I believe God finally heard me. I was only two years old, but I remember this particular night oh so well. My foster mom was getting ready to give me my usual bath, but this time she meant for me to drown and burn me to death. I remember hearing her say these words. "You will never be anything and never have been. I see why your parents gave you up."

I reached for her legs to try to calm her down, hoping that clinging to her leg would change her mind—it didn't work. She grabbed me by my hair and dragged me to the bath. I didn't know exactly what hot water felt like, but I quickly found out. She dumped me in the water and I sat there crying, two years old, barely able to save myself, barely able to mumble a word. The last thing I remember was being burnt all over my body. She threw back a loud laugh and enjoyed every minute of my suffering. I clearly remember a light that was really bright as I slowly began dying. All of a sudden the lights went away. When I woke up I was in a hospital in Memphis, Tennessee. I saw machines everywhere, but I never saw her again. I was treated like a little princess while I was in the hospital. I was in what I called "Children's heaven." I was fed, treated with love, actually talked to and not talked at. This is a telling picture of my life and the pain that has haunted me to this day.

I didn't know why I had to endure that at such a young age, or why anyone would make me suffer and laugh about it. The flashback feels so real. I spent countless hours crying, questioning, and wondering about the unknown. I began to fear the same thing happening again, at any moment. Every time I lay down to sleep, all I could see was the flashback haunting me until I finally was old enough to ask God for revelation and understanding of that night. I wanted answers to my entire list of questions, but I forgot to acknowledge that I was only two, with no way of protecting myself. I began to finally see that light I saw as God's presence at such a young age. I saw that flashback become a greater strength and testimony for my life. I started to smile just because I was able to wake up and eat real food.

(Tameka at age three with her adopted mother)

It wasn't easy, transferring my life from a mother that cared nothing for me to a single mother that gave up everything to adopt me. I cried every night and every time I woke up. I was quiet as a little girl. No one knew the real reason I was crying; no one knew the reason I didn't really eat. You see, after being adopted, I tried to throw my flashbacks to the side, ignoring them and crying alone. I never spoke of my pain because it was too unbearable. I truly didn't see why I was allowed to enter a place of so much suffering, just to turn around and be placed in a family that really loved and took me in. I didn't understand it to the point of resisting the thought process.

I fought my mom. I wouldn't allow her to get close to me. I blocked a mother and daughter bond, because inside I could feel and see that lady that called herself "Mom" once before. You see, I experienced this trauma but I didn't truly accept it like I should have. God was there when I couldn't protect myself. He held me in my mother's womb and all the way to that nightmare. My question was why – God, why did I have to go through all of that just to get here? God, why is it that I can't find purpose in my pain? God threw a question back to me that honestly I didn't have an answer to.

Why have you doubted me in your life? I heard him say, *My child, you have a purpose to fulfill. Stop questioning me. Embrace your testimony. Embrace what I brought you through. You love hard because you never felt the love you've been searching for. You fell hard because you gave all your energy and love to the wrong people.* He continued, saying, *I challenge you to let all your pain turn into my glory, and I'll show you what real love is. Now it is time for you to stop questioning me and my love for you and walk in your faith, because I have never left your side, and I never will. Many people do not understand you because they don't really know you. All they know is that smile that you put on underneath your pain and insecurities.*

I realized that just like God was there for me when I didn't know Him there was no way He would fail me now.

How many understand that God knows us before we ever know Him? I didn't know why I doubted God and saw my life as worthless, but I have a slight idea. I have many scars but they have truly worked for my good. I am so glad I made it this far. To God be all the glory and praise because without Him I would be nothing! I had to open my eyes to the reality that there is purpose in everything that had been taken in my life. If you stay connected to God, no matter who you are or what you are going through, God will see you through! Even though your story and life's trails are not mine, I have come to tell you from experience that purpose is following you, strength is coming to you, divine favor is blessing you, and God is ready to direct you!

I know that many of you, like me, have buried so much pain in your hearts and minds even when you knew God was there holding your hands. I started to see my life and struggles as worthless. I also started to constantly dwell on the negative and the past rather than the bright future God had planned for my life. The devil comes to our lives to do three things—to steal our minds, destroy our hearts, and kill our souls. The devil knows our true purpose before we do, because he too had the honor of the same purpose. That was to walk in the will and light of God. It's not always easy to embrace the pain because pain is a scary sense of falsehood of what death can be. Pain can be described as a feeling triggered in the nervous system. It may be sharp or dull. It may come and go or it can be constant. Pain can be helpful in diagnosing a problem through God's will.

I want you to think back to that person, place, or thing that triggers your pain. This time I want you to thank God for that pain because our pain leads us to increase our faith. This led me to the verse in the Bible, "It is good for me that I was afflicted, that I may learn your statutes" (Psalm 119:71). Our pain leads us to cry out God's name. It leads us to standing on our needs, praying prayers we never thought we had the power or authority to pray. That pain leads us to what the right way is and it shows us our flaws. That pain presents our weaknesses as well as our strengths. That pain calls us to our true destiny in God.

How many times have you been in so much pain and all you wanted to do was get rid of a little of that throbbing thrown at your heart, mind, body or even soul? When we get sick, we tend to avoid the doctor's office because we feel we can get through it on our own. We tend to push it back and not call anyone for help. When we start to feel the pain and begin to see what has triggered it, we start to seek a solution, whether that is some type of medicine or an adjustment in our lifestyle. We begin to move to the hospital where we know as a place sick people go, right? Well, that's what we also do spiritually. We go to church when we need a higher solution to our pain and our problems. We seek to find answers to relate all that hurt that causes the pain we are feeling. The Word of God becomes our medicine. Our tears and prayers become our therapy for getting and recovering from that problem, that pain. We continue to go Sunday after Sunday, worshipping God a little more every time. We begin to stop caring who sees us hurting. We stop caring who the patients in the room are. We just want to stop our pain and get rid of our problem. This begins a domino effect, and begins a thirst for the divine doctor and his prescriptions. God is our doctor. If it wasn't for pain we would never see our doctor, talk to our doctor, and even at times cry to our doctor. We will never get our written prescription to our lifestyle of pain.

Without going through pain, we will never understand the concept of healing, delivery, and restoration. We will never know that we are not alone, that we have a doctor who cannot only take care of our problems but the problems of those we have prayed for. Consider this – without the pain and the side effects of some of the types of medicines we have tried to take in spite of that what God, our true doctor prescribes, we will never open up our eyes. We will never see how miracles are forming, how people who are sick suddenly get well. We will continue to go through life without a care in the world. Constantly ruining and poisoning our lives. We are constantly letting the devil deceive us and our loved ones. We would never pick up the Bible for answers. We would never know how powerful and good our God really is.

That pain we feel is what we should start to embrace. I know when you went back to that day, time and place where your pain started you can say that if it wasn't for the Lord, you would still be in that same place, feeling that same pain. You know for a fact that the pain you felt actually didn't hinder your life, but rather it saved it, as well as the life of many others around you. So do not let the pain, whatever type it is, control you. Grab hold and take control of it.

Ever heard of tough love? When you know your life is not pleasing to the ones around you, even though you think you are having a ball, you start to feel lonely and down. You start to realize what's important in your life and what truly matters. You look at that addiction, person, place, or thing, and begin to say:

> "No more. No more will I let you change my mood when my day is going fine. No more will I please you because I want to avoid a conflict with you. No more will I worship you. And no more will I blame myself. No more will I allow you to steal my happiness, my joy, strength, and life."

Tough love will help you see things you were too stubborn to realize and too blind to see for yourself. That is the way with God. He gives us tough love at times and allows the devil to knock us down so He can begin to build us up again. "No discipline is enjoyable while it is happening. It's painful! But afterward there will be a peaceful harvest of right living for those who are trained in this way" (Hebrews 12:11).

God will allow the devil to come between our relationships so that we can see that He has something better for us. He allows the devil to get in our minds so that we can start to see that our negative thoughts have controlled our lives over and over again. He doesn't do this to hurt us, but to bring us to a place where all we can do is deny ourselves, latch onto Jesus, our faith, and God's Word, and walk in it. He lets us understand that He is in control regardless of what the devil throws at us. This tough love is what our brain knows as *pain*. We have to suffer, to struggle. We must endure pain time after time. God makes no mistakes, but doesn't put on us more than He knows we can bear.

Why do you constantly run for those things that trigger your heart? Why do you give up when things get tough when you know God promised He would walk with you through the valley of the shadow of death? Why do you continue to pity your sorrow and call on people for answers just to only feel more pain? It is time for us to get back on track and stop letting the devil cause our sickness, in whatever form that may be. It's time for us to stop looking back and focus more on looking forward. It's time to let God direct our paths and our minds. Stop letting the devil have the satisfaction that he is getting to us. Should it take a dramatic situation to happen for us to get our life right with God? Does he have to kill us spiritually before we realize our life is worthless without Him? Do we have to continue to see our brothers and sisters cry and hurt? Does it take us losing our loved ones to get the picture? Does it take a minister to constantly instill the same promise for our life from God before we truly understand? It's sad that we constantly fight each other but do not fight the demons that are warring among us every day.

I remember when God spoke to me and said, *We all have gifts instilled in us because we were made in His image.* I would seek to find my gift, trying everything I thought it could be when it was with me all along. It was my ability to feel others' pain. When I was able to stand strong when others broke, it was because of the authority He placed in my life through my passion for writing and speaking. Do not make up excuses and tell God you're not available to be used because your life isn't together. God doesn't want to hear that you have to live for yourself first, or that you have to do what you want before you obey His word. God is a God of fairness and justice.

You may think that as long as you have been fighting God's purpose and thriving through His gifts, you haven't seen anything going as you planned. You might see your life crumbling and see yourself crying tears you thought had passed by. Now you constantly see answers that you were too blind to see when God first revealed them to you. When God calls you, listen and just say *yes*. Accept the confirmation and embrace your gifts and talents. So what if you have messed up? That doesn't make God love you any less. So what if people constantly talk about what you used to do? You should stand strong with God's purpose and promise, and look at your own life, not those of others. I think our problems are not so much that we constantly blame the devil, but rather that we blame ourselves and God. "But the Lord said to me, Do not say, I am only a youth, for to all whom I send you, you shall go, and whatever I command you, you shall speak. Do not be afraid of them, for I am with you to deliver you, declares the Lord" (Jeremiah 1:7-8).

I will tell you a little about me. I'm a girl who was fighting her calling and promise for life. I'm a girl who made mistake after mistake. I'm a girl who has been abused, talked about, and scorned. I'm a girl who didn't know how to find her way back to the cross. I'm a girl that has been through hell and back again. I'm a girl who hurt many people because I didn't always want to do the right thing. I'm a girl who has let my pain control me, day in and day out. I'm a girl who failed to realize how blessed I was and how God took care of me. I'm a girl who has had to start over and be broken down, one last time, to hear God's voice again. I'm that girl that loved hard and got hurt in the process. I'm that girl that constantly blamed herself for what has happened to her. But how many know God is a God of faithfulness, grace, and mercy?

He picked my head up on January 25, 2013. I'm that same girl he gave a second chance. That girl who knew my purpose and calling but refused to be chosen until that night, where God spoke not in parables but clearly. He called me to speak of my story to let my pain I was going through turn into that miracle and blessing many needed to hear. God told me that it wasn't too late to say *yes*, that I am wholeheartedly following Him all the way to heaven. He told me that my time is now to speak of the many testimonies I have. It was time for me to give Him the glory through my story and stop giving the devil the glory through my life. He said, *If you say yes tonight and mean it, I will give you back everything you thought the devil stole from you. I will give you the ability to love hard again. The peace you've been searching for. The happiness you cried for. I will give you a sound mind back. I will give you your anointing back.*

I remember walking down to the altar and lifting my hands to God, saying I couldn't do this alone. I pointed out that I couldn't continue to live my life without Him and His purpose. I remember telling God "yes" over and over again, as He flashed my life back before my eyes. I saw my pain overcome by His peace. I saw, for the first time, with my eyes open. I had been running from person to person, seeking help when God was there all along. I had been carrying my baggage since foster care. Remembering over and over again, the beatings I received, the words that had been spoken to me, telling me I never was anything and I never would be. I saw God's revelation and confirmation come to pass as I thought about everything that had taken place throughout my life.

I began to once again have a thirst for His way and His will. I could once again feel His true anointing enter my life. I understood for the first time in a long time that He gave me a second chance, not for me to continue to live for me and my way, but for Him and His. I heard Him say, *It is done.* I felt a joy that I never thought I would feel again. I heard Him say, *No more will you be defeated for you are victorious.* All I could do was cry and fall to my knees because I realized in that moment how real God really was. You will never truly get that encounter until you seek God's voice, when you can remove all distractions. What is your confirmation? How much do you want to be able to walk again and not worry about fainting? To die in yourself so you might live in Him? How much do you want to see God reveal his confirmation in your life?

Can you just close your eyes and begin to hear God speak to you? Can you begin to hear his revelation and promise, just like

I did? I'm telling you - if he can use a weak, scared, broken girl, and turn her into a wise, strong, determined, anointed vessel in Him, He can do the same for you. No, I don't know why it took me so long to realize that God was calling my name (even as a teen), but I know that from that day - January 25, 2013 - I have said "yes", and don't plan to change that.

Some of you right now are in the same position that I was back then. You have tried everything you could think of as your solution, which turned out to be only temporary. Why not do us both a favor and try God? He has called many but few are chosen – those are the words that will forever rest in my heart, because to be chosen means to say "yes" and stop running from that calling, which is one of the greatest gifts one can receive. Just as God gave us things in life, he can surely take them away. Our world is dying and if we don't start being *in* the world but not *of* the world, souls that are crying out will not be saved. People will not be healed. People will never be set free.

The world is going to hell and we are the ones who are Christians, called to speak boldly God's name. To tell the world their sins are forgiven because Jesus Christ, who knew his purpose on this Earth and accepted his confirmation, walked in it, no matter what people said or did to him, praying for strength in God and guidance. He paved the way for us all so that the sins we committed can be forgiven and we can still be used by God. What if Jesus shad aid no over and over again? There is no telling what would have happened. If God kept calling him to preach, minister, and teach and he instead said, "Yes God, but wait. God

I'm comfortable right now. I don't want to change positions. Maybe later, I'll go." If Jesus didn't say *yes* none of us would have a place to go where there is no more pain. We would not have a place to run to when the pain gets too unbearable. When Jesus declared, *yes*, God allowed him to suffer, but prepared Jesus' heart and mind so that his purpose could be fulfilled. We suffer to come to that place in God where all He can do is lead us the way to His light. God does not want us to continue to doubt him. He does not want us to continue to be hateful and mean to our fellow brothers and sisters. God called us to love one another just as Christ loved us.

If you truly love God and want to be blessed, you will start to walk in the promises of God. You will start to cry out for your brothers and sisters in Christ. God does not take us through things in vain. Everything we do and everything we go through is a test and preparation for the final exam.

It is up to you and me to decide if we want to make his promises come to pass in our lives or not. You do not have to preach to be used by God and bring souls to him. You can merely be a listening ear for someone. You can be that smile or laugh they needed that day. You can be that angel that prays and cries on their behalf. You can be that hand that helps them hold on. You can be that miracle for their life and situation through your lifestyle and attitude, knowing that in spite of what you have been through you are still reaching for a higher place and God. That you are still calling on God and worshipping him every chance you get.

God is real - if you do not believe it, think back to that thing that caused your pain. How did you get to that point of peace? How were you able to overcome it over and over again? Why doesn't it affect you like it used to? How are you able to forgive that person in spite of the horrible things they did and said to you? It's not you alone, but God that lives in you. If you know God is real then I ask you to start acting like it. Seek him more. Love him harder; trust him beyond your situation. God knows I had to. God will not let you down. He will not let you get to a place and just leave you. You have to be willing to take that step in faith and tell Him it's no longer your way, but His. If you start saying yes to God and no to the devil, your life will change in a dramatic way. You will see just how real and true God really is.

I learned three things through my encounter with God. First, the sin in pride. Pride is probably the biggest downfall we have as humans. When God instructs us to do something that is uncomfortable or unpopular in our reputational status, we get so caught up in our titles that we miss the blessing that God designed. I was so caught up in my age, gender, and race that I didn't want to be used by God. I did not want to admit my mistakes and dark times. My pride wanted me to be seen as the confident person, not the one that was weak and insecure at times. I was so focused on my human and fleshly abilities that I failed to see that God wanted to use me for His glory. We have become too prideful, caught up in our reputations and ourselves that we will not allow God to use us to be a blessing to someone else. Pride stops the purpose of God. I learned that pride is what

Satan uses to keep us from stepping out of our comfortable state and our will, rather than stepping in God's purpose and His will for our lives. "One's pride will bring him low, but he who is lowly in spirit will obtain honor" (Proverbs 29:3).

Second, I learned that the devil can't kill what God has anointed to live. We are too busy complaining about our lives and wishing our problems away that we cannot grasp God's signs of our anointing. God has his hands on our lives. The devil has perhaps tried to take you on several occasions, and you wonder why you are still here. God told me to tell you it's because you have a purpose to live. You weren't born as a mistake, but for a promise in His name. Sometimes God allows the devil to attack us to get our full attention and get our mind back on track. We have to start seeking the truth and not the worldly things. The things of the world will only kill us if we allow them to overcome us. Finally, God told me that fear stops our miracles. Fear is the faith in the devil – true faith is faith in God. If we aren't careful we will get too caught up in what the devil can do more than what God has the power and authority to do.

The devil does not have any power until we allow him to have it. God never allows pain without a purpose in the lives of His children. He never allows Satan, or circumstances, or any ill-intending person to afflict us unless He uses that affliction for our good. God never wastes pain. He always causes it to work together for our ultimate good, the good of conforming us more to the likeness of His Son.

I ask God, right now, to come into your heart and mind

and reveal to you an understanding above any other. God uses people we know to get the message across if we are too blind to see it for ourselves. I ask God, right now, to remove the spirit of fear and uncertainty and replace it with power, authority, and certainty. We are all called by God in one way or the other as we live our lives. You may not be called to be a preacher. You may be called to be a living witness so that someone who needs to hear the miracles God has performed in our lives may do so.

Maybe He called you to forgiveness so that your sins can be forgiven. Maybe he has called you to worship Him when you have had too much pride in the past, and you have missed out on your blessings over and over again. Maybe He is calling you to stop and listen to His plans for your life and not the plans of your parents, your friends, your enemies or even yourself. Let God be first in your life in everything you do. I am a living testimony that if you ignore what God is saying to you, pain and confusion will continue to rule your mind, body, and soul.

Maybe you were, like me, afraid to let God use you because of the mistakes you have made in the past or how broken you think and feel you are. Maybe you don't feel God has seen the tears you have cried over and over again. I come to tell you that you are not alone in anything you do. Let your pain and struggles become your pride and joy, because you are still here. In God, we have our being. Stop allowing the devil to steal your joy and decrease your faith. Let the devil know he is not welcome at all.

I had to learn the hard way that everyone was not my friend, but that in Jesus I had a true friend who did not come to destroy and kill my promise but to help it come to pass. Remember, God can fix whatever is broken.

It's not over until God says it's over. One last thing – do not accept your calling for fashion and show (this is pride), but deny yourself and save the souls of the lost. For whom the Son sets free is truly free indeed. If you are sick of being sick and tired, then make the choice to follow Jesus. Remember that only what we do for Christ will last.

I have always been told that it profits a man nothing to gain the whole world and lose his soul. Young people like me are dying back to back, and that in itself it should be a wakeup call to not just my generation, but every generation to come.

I want you to know that before you enter into the next chapter God wants to turn all your pain, hurt, and anger to the greater destiny He has for you, but you must position yourself and your life. You have to say:

"Lord, I need more and want more of you. I need your power, God, in the midst of my pain and mess. I want to see your glory shine in my life. God, less of me and more of you is what I ultimately need. God, the world is not where I want to dwell anymore, but God I want to dwell in your love and warm embrace again."

Tell God right now you are going to stop blaming Him and walk boldly in power and might under His authority. Stop speaking negatively. I had to see that everything that looks good in the world does not always bear the best fruit or harvest.

Yes, there are times when a snake will bite, but God has the power to pull the hand of that snake back from your life and say "No more!" You are a child of the King, You deserve the best and nothing less. I challenge you not to settle because you are exhausted. Do like I had to do—stop doubting God and walk in your faith!

Chapter 4

What Do I Do Now, God?

Psalms 13

How long, LORD? Will you forget me forever?
How long will you hide your face from me?
² How long must I wrestle with my thoughts
and day after day have sorrow in my heart?
How long will my enemy triumph over me?
³ Look on me and answer, LORD my God.
Give light to my eyes, or I will sleep in death,
⁴ and my enemy will say, "I have overcome him,"
and my foes will rejoice when I fall.
⁵ But I trust in your unfailing love
my heart rejoices in your salvation.
⁶ I will sing the LORD's praise,
for He has been good to me.

I sat upright on my bed and cried my eyes out, because that morning I was sexually assaulted by a guy that I looked up to. Many associate the word sexual assault with rape, however that was not the case. According to the United States Department of Justice, the definition of sexual assault is *any type of sexual contact or behavior that occurs without the explicit consent of the recipient, even fondling*. Falling under the definition of sexual assault are sexual activities as forced.

I told him everything about myself, hoping that he would learn to trust me like a "little sister." I kept going back to the text message that I took as a joke right before the assault took place. That morning I needed to run a few errands off campus, and I didn't know who else to call but my "big brother." I'll call him King No Name. He answered as quickly as he normally did when I needed to take a trip off campus. I was all bubbly and happy to be spending time with him again.

I was getting ready when my best friend who was lying beside my phone, said, "Your brother texted you."

I put the code in my phone and scrolled through my Inbox to see if he had maybe changed his mind and I would have find another ride. Shockingly the message read, "Are you going to give me some head money?" I didn't understand what he meant by this. I was a freshman in college and I wasn't very street smart. I knew that he played around a lot and I really didn't take it as seriously as I should have. I responded by saying, "I can give you gas money, but I don't understand what you mean by head money." He replied, "I was joking. Don't worry about it. I'm on my way, be ready."

I looked at my best friend and told her what he texted to me. She looked back at me and said, "Are you sure he was playing?" I said, "Yes, of course he was. He wouldn't force me to do anything, right?"

I began to imagine his words as he pulled up to my dorm in his car. He had the biggest smile on his face, as though he was happy to be spending time with me. I pushed my worries to the back of my head and hopped in the front seat. Our plans were to go to the Superdome because I needed to get my PASS to work for the upcoming game. As we were riding down by the Superdome, I got a weird vibe that I have never had before. It was as if I knew something wasn't right, but just didn't know what.

I proceeded to get out of the car once he stopped, and he got out and followed me to the elevator. While riding the elevator, he said, "You know you're going to have to give me some head money for doing this, right?" I remained quiet as if he didn't say what I knew he did, and then proceeded to walk into the building. There was a long line and the man told me to have a seat and make sure I had my ID ready for my picture to be taken. He told King No Name that he couldn't go with me because he wasn't the one working, so he stayed in the café.

As I was sitting in my seat waiting to be called for my picture, all types of things fluttered through my head. I wanted to know why I put myself in this situation. I trusted someone and let them get close to me, and now I was stuck. I was with this person who had already said things to me that I knew weren't right. At one point I told myself that I was overthinking everything, and nothing was going to happen to me. He was my play brother, right? The one I viewed as family in my eyes. Why would I think he would hurt me? That was the question that rang in my head.

After I was done getting my PASS for work, I went to where King No Name was. He said to me, "You left me all alone. You really owe me now."

At this point I was fed up with being threatened by him and being disrespected. So I looked him in the face and said, "No, I don't like you like that. You are my brother, my family, stop asking me for head money."

He got quiet and said," You don't know how to have fun. I was just joking."

I rolled my eyes. We walked back to the car and headed to Walmart. I remember a voice telling me I was in danger, and that I needed to remove myself. I ignored that voice and I sat in the car until we arrived at Walmart. I got out, grabbed all my belongings and went inside. King No Name decided he wanted to stay in the car.

I was in Walmart getting everything I thought I needed and wanted at the time. In other words, trying to be a normal college girl. I was getting in line when King No Name called me on my cell phone and said, "Come on, I'm tired of sitting in the car." So, being the person I am, always giving someone the benefit of the doubt, I rushed back outside. I noticed that he was parked far from the Walmart entrance. I didn't think anything about it. I put the items in the car, got back in the front seat, and proceeded to put on my seatbelt.

King No Name turned off the car. He looked at me and said, "Are you ready?"

At that time, I knew what he was referring to. I said, "I am engaged. I do not like you like that and will not give you oral sex. I just want to go back to the dorm." I threatened to call his girlfriend, who was my big sister on campus, and the only reason I trusted him at all.

He said, "Who do you think she will believe? Me or you?" He repeated that I owed him.

At this point, my first move should have been to get out of the car, but I sat there, frozen, not knowing what to do.

King No Name said, "This will be better practice for your fiancé. I'm sure he will love it more."

I think that was the moment when it hit me. I must put my foot down. I yelled, "LEAVE ME ALONE!"

He insisted on something happening so he reached for my pants. "Well, let me finger you and you give me a hand job." He took out his penis. "Come on, just make me cum." He moved his hands toward my neck and tried to force me into an oral sex position.

I pushed his hand back and said, "Stop, what is wrong with you? Just take me back to the dorm. I don't like this." I told him that I would tell his girlfriend when we got back to campus if he didn't stop.

He finally gave up and started the car. The whole way back no words were exchanged. I felt disgusted and confused. I didn't understand why he was trying to get in my pants. I just kept thinking back to who I thought he was versus who he actually turned out to be. He dropped me off at my dorm as if nothing had happened, and I knew he expected me to be quiet about everything, but I couldn't. I went back to my room and was so traumatized by what had happened as it replayed over and over in my head. I reflected back to all the signs that I ignored and missed before the situation happened. I had so many thoughts that went through my head, all the *whys, hows,* and *what fors.* I didn't understand why I had allowed myself to be placed in that position. I blamed myself for everything and did everything I could to try to erase him from my head. Still, I had to talk to someone, and the first person I spoke with was my then-mentor on campus. She made me realize that I hadn't done anything wrong, but I was in the wrong place at the wrong time. To think that he would do me that way made me want to reevaluate everyone that supposedly loved me and wanted the best for my life.

I hid the pain inside. I didn't want anyone to know what I had just faced. I was never seen as one that would get trapped and fooled. I was always the strong person and the independent warrior. This broke me down. I began to lose myself - my joy, my pride, my identity. I had never encountered or faced such a terrible time in my life.

The Martin Luther King, Jr. holiday turned me into a weak, confused, angry person. I turned cold, hardened to anyone that looked at me. I shut everything out and I tried to guard my life. Still I was miserable. I found myself sick all the time. I kept trying to escape any memory of my past experiences, from abuse to bad relationships in the past.

I couldn't go to Walmart without taking that encounter along with me. I couldn't see anyone that I knew was connected to him. I found myself almost hating anything that resembled him and I felt betrayed by anyone that called themselves my friends but still interacted with him in anyway. I began to walk in fear on campus. Even though I prayed to God, I felt he could no longer hear me. I felt unclean and disgusted. I watched day and night for a miracle to take place in my life, but nothing happened. I resented God more and more when I saw King No Name anywhere on campus.

I went through a "David's cry out" in my life, during my first year of college. I cried out so much to God in anger that I thought I would run out of tears. "I am worn out from my groaning. All night long I flood my bed with weeping and drench my couch with tears." (Psalm 6:6) I felt like David in that I cried to the point of soaking my pillow. I went through the experience like never before: the traumatic experience of being sexually assaulted.

Like 80 to 90% of college sexual assault victims, I knew the person that sexually assaulted me.* Like I previously stated, I looked up to him and loved him dearly like a brother; however, he had other plans.

I felt trapped on campus, feeling like I was nothing, and he had won the battle over me. I was so hurt that I went into a state of depression and silence. I didn't talk to anyone because he was in a fraternity and he had just crossed over to receive his letters. I can't begin to tell you how I felt around this time. I felt the world was against me, and no one would believe anything I said. I felt intimidated and confused at how I even allowed it to happen to me. I didn't feel that anyone would or could understand the pain I was dealing with. I had every emotion possible run through my head: anger, regret, frustration, and bitterness. This guy was going to be able to freely live his life as if what happened to me was ok, and I should have just kept my mouth shut. I felt that eyes of judgment were following everywhere I went. I was the one forced to go to counseling, and every day I went, it made me feel worse. I felt I was being pacified to keep his name on campus good, yet my name was being destroyed. I feared him, and I was disgusted every time I heard his name. The reason I feared him the most was because I was afraid of what else he was going to do to me. He had sent me a threatening text message once I told and he found out. Another reason I feared him was because he knew almost everyone on campus and he was pretty popular. I felt he could ruin my life and reputation. It was again my word against his, and I had never been in that situation before.

He destroyed my relationship with his girlfriend who was like a big sister to me. All of his close friends were in some type of leadership positions on campus. I felt there was no place I could go without running into one of his friends – therefore, I refused to go anywhere on campus, save for quick trips to class and back to my room. No one really knew why I was silent and shut out but his people and my close friends. I was no longer an outgoing type of person, but the more reserved and observed type. I didn't know who to run and talk to about it but God.

I believe the hardest decision I had to make was to press

campus charges or press federal charges. I went with the campus charges, not because it happened on campus because it did not, but he was a student and I just wanted him to understand what he did to me wasn't right. I didn't want to ruin his life, send him to prison with a sex offender charge. I just wanted him to serve some type of consequence for his actions toward me. The reason I pressed charges at all was because I knew that if I didn't someone else could have been a victim; and I wanted the guy to see that what he did wasn't a minor mistake. Once I proceeded to make campus charges against him, I was forced to tell the same story over and over again to a lot of people in charge. Every time I had to repeat it, it was like living the experience all over again.

Throughout all of this, God worked things out on my behalf. The day came and they called me from class for the hearing. I was terrified because I didn't want to be placed in a room all alone with people that I didn't know anything about. I asked my best friend what I should do and we prayed straight through the waiting period until it was my time to speak. She wasn't allowed to go back to the room with me but she stood by me and I was thankful for that. My close friends also came to support me and they wrote witness letters and were rooting for me to win the case.

I began to walk back to the room and I heard God say, *I got this, just speak.* So I sat down with about twelve faculty members and my work-study boss. My heart sank. No matter how much I wanted to turn around and forget it all, I closed my eyes and prayed as they spoke the charges. Right when I was starting to talk, all the lights went out. I knew then God was in the room and that was his sign for me. I no longer had to see their faces and all the audio recording devices, but I saw an angel appear in the dark with a smile, then the lights turned on again and all my worry was gone. I was filled with peace. No one intimidated me anymore. I spoke and I saw just how quickly God moved. Various people threw cross-examining questions my way, but the truth and God covered and protected me. The conclusion was that he was guilty and I was free to go. Don't get me wrong - I didn't want to get this guy in big trouble so I didn't file a police report. God gave me a peace and a forgiving spirit therefore, it was not my intentions to ruin his life, just let him understand that it was not okay what he did to me.

I realized in the midst of it all God gave me a new strength and understanding of life. Let me explain. Even though the guy was a student on campus doesn't mean the university didn't take precautions against sexual assault. Many times we blame the university or ourselves for allowing the thing to happen, but the truth of the matter is you can't stop what you don't anticipate happening. I allowed this to happen because I never expected the results to be as they were. Just as many victims on college campuses, it destroyed my trust.

I realized that no matter how much a college expresses the intolerance of sexual assault or harassment, it still can and will occur. It was hard being on that campus for a long time, but after I came to the conclusion that my university had no way of stopping the assault, that's when I was truly free. As long as a victim has the mindset that the university is against them, they will never be truly free to live a peaceful and joyful life. The key to freeing my mind was forgiving for myself.

Yes, I wish I could have gotten the apology I was seeking, but I got something better - I got a voice. Not any voice, but God's. I went back to my room and I heard God say, *Satan is not winning, you have to stop looking back and move forward with me...are you ready now? Are you ready for your new look?* I was confused and didn't know exactly what it all meant, but I knew I was going to make it and get back to being me. By the grace and mercy of God's unfailing love, I finished my first year at Xavier with a high GPA.

I discovered who God was and how I had for too long demanded want I wanted out of life, and not what He did. I didn't pick my friends wisely. I didn't listen to God when He told me to stay away from that guy. I took a chance on my own life and invited the devil in without caution. I'm not revealing this testimony to make the guy on campus look bad, and I am not excusing what he did, but I thank God for allowing me to go through that because I learned through that pain that God is also in the trenches of life. I sought God like never before and I finally found Him. I finally knew what I should do after that trial.

I learned how to stand firm on my faith and be hidden in God's presence. I began to see how real God was in my life, but I still had the questions of what to do next. He led me to the passage in the Bible about David, which was Psalms 13. I was too busy wondering how long the process was going to take, and in suffering alone I forgot about God's unfailing love and His promises over my life, just like David in the Bible. God was preparing me for my greater purpose that was coming - the greater power I received through His anointing, and a relationship with God! I was already made in Jesus' name!

As I began to analyze this Biblical passage, I understood what David was going through. I could see David standing, crying out to God, repeating the words "how long" over and over again until he could hear the answer revealed from God. God does things his way, in his own time and place. He is not looking at our planner or our slightest directions in life. He is looking at the end result: our true destiny He searches our heart day and night and knocks quietly, trying to get our attention and keep us from the destruction that we cannot see is taking place.

David began the journey of God as a young boy. He was forced to experience the good and the bad so his purpose could one day be fulfilled. Sometimes to get to God's true purpose for our lives we have to endure the frightening and rough circumstances. We need something to prepare us for that final exam that we have to take to enter the kingdom of God. We cannot enter the kingdom if we are not ready. If we would rather hold on to the past and the baggage then we cannot see where God is trying to lead us, and we tend to become blind to our own reality.

(Tameka, age 4)

I used to wonder why, when I was younger, I would constantly get caught whenever I was doing the wrong things. It seemed like everyone else around me could do the same action and it was as if the light was so dark that not even I could see that they were doing wrong. I don't dwell on the beatings or whippings I received as a child because though I might have hurt and was brought to anger in the moment, it helped me transform into a better person and mature woman. It has helped me to understand God a little bit more, at a deeper level.

You remember the saying your mom, dad, or authority figure would say right before that punishment or whipping you receive - "This is going to hurt me more than its going hurt you?" I used to see that as foolishness and I couldn't wrap that around my little mind. How in the world was this going to hurt them more, when they were the one with the belt in their hand and I was down here stretched out?

Bear with me as I take you farther. Please don't miss this. Take yourself back to that day when you discovered what the word *sin* really meant. You probably felt like me - guilty, confused, and even at times misunderstood, right? You saw sin as hideous in your life and you knew that you were doing nothing but living in darkness, right? But one day came where you learned about forgiveness, repentance, and confession which led you straight to salvation and a man by the name of Jesus that saved you from your sins over and over again, no matter what sin you committed.

God is our authority. He is just the last one we have to answer to. When we commit a sin or do something wrong we get punished and whipped by God even harder. My mom was a very firm and strict lady. When she spoke and wanted something done it was said and done. She didn't play that whole talk back to me and do your own thing. No matter what my plans were in the midst of it all, I learned that I had stop my own thoughts and actions to follow my mom because she was my provider of strength. She was watching over me, holding my hand as child. How dare I disrespect such a powerful lady of God. She taught me that life was never going to be easy without the Lord - we had to follow His will and His way before our own. I could see that when I chose to either tune her words out or just do my own thing, I fell much harder. I cried a little bit longer, and it hurt just a little bit more.

God is our father - He is our provider and protector, right? He watches over us as adults when no else is there. He talks with us and to us night and day. Why is it that we constantly tune Him out? That we constantly truly believe our way of life is the best way? Why do we disrespect Him and His Word? Is it because we are seeking our own pleasures? Is it because we want to shine in the lime light? God is not pleased with us switching His words around to fit our lifestyle or our own pleasures. Now think for a moment, are we really naturally patient human beings? Do we like to wait in line for our miracles or blessings, or are we 'right now' type of people? We should not allow ourselves to put time limits on the move and work of God.

Our respect for God's Words knows no age limit, even if a more genuine understanding of His truth might come at a later age. God, how long? Time can be a scary factor in life because we constantly measure our own happiness with time. If we are younger in age and God instructs a task we never experienced before, we tend to reject the assignment or calling and tell God, "I'm too young right now. My life is just not together. Can you use me in a few more years? Can you just skip me this time and come back again? God, I'm just not ready. I am just not where I feel you need me to be. God, I'm still trying to party and have fun. I'm not ready for adult responsibility, so please come back to me later. Think about it for a minute - your Father has instructed you with a task and your reply to Him is come back to me. No ma'am, no sir, that is just outright crazy.

God lets you have your freedom for a little while, but He knows you cannot handle it or even breathe without Him. Seeing that you don't quite understand it, He decides He is going to step back and let you do His job in your own life. No matter how much I sometimes couldn't stand my mom's rules I had to follow them. But it came to the point where I started to tune her so far out that she gave up on me. It brings up bad memories when a father or mother give up on their child. It's a problem for me when you can't see what is right from what's wrong. You can't understand that your life needs a turnaround in a hurry.

Have you ever disappointed your loved one so badly that they were simply silent in their disappointment? And in silence comes confusion and frustration, because you want to know how they have been wronged so you can make it right. You want to know that they still care, but can't tell because they are silent. You are now in a place where you need direction and instruction. After following your own plans, you later find out that mama and daddy were right all along. So now you're mad because you've made a mistake, and you're wondering to God, "What happened? Where did it all go wrong?" In the midst of this little war of temptation and mistakes, the devil grabs your mind and fills it with negativity and you start to question everything, even your own purpose and life.

You are now crying out to everyone, trying to figure out

what happened. Trying to see why you didn't catch the signs and warnings. So now you are all alone and can't find a friend. You can't find any joy, and you can't find God. You've been calling God, asking where He is, that He's too silent right now when you need Him to confront you. You might be saying,

"God, I'm tired of my way. I want to try yours because I've messed up and I don't know what to do. God, haven't you seen my tears and my pain? Haven't you heard what happened to me? God, where are you? I need to know what to do. I am running out of time. God, how long? I am losing my patience, God. How long? How long must I suffer for my mistakes? How long must I face these tears and this pain? God, how long? I am ready to give up and I am ready to escape. I don't like reality, God. I don't like seeing myself turn in circles to land at the same spot every single time. How long, God. Can you hear me? Do you care? God, I need you. How long?

As we cry out to God and we can't seem to hear His answer, we begin to curse and question His existence. We begin to rethink our beliefs and our own strength and faith. We question if God really is there. Because we can't see Him, and we surely can't hear Him, we stop and drop our heads in shame, pretending that we have it all together. When our parent punishes us we tend to want to know how long this whipping will last or how long we will be without something. We need to know when the punishment will end. How long, two weeks? Months? A year?

We can't bear not to know. And, if you had parents like mine that just wouldn't let me know how long, but tell me that "it's not over till the fat lady sings," then you tend to forget that you've now tuned God out and are unwilling to hear Him through your pain.

I remember once, I made my mom so angry that she punished me by making me ride the bus, and Lord knows I couldn't stand riding the bus. It came with a price. I had to get up earlier than normal. I didn't see her as much and we didn't communicate too well. My friends would ask me how long she was making me ride the bus. I looked at them and said that I didn't know because she wouldn't tell me. I only knew that I hated riding the bus. I hated getting up and losing just a little bit of sleep, and I hated the miscommunication that came along with the punishment.

Now, just like my mom made me ride the bus - something I couldn't stand - God makes us own up and face our own reality, which to be sure, is not the first action that we want to take place. We want to ride comfortably, where we are safe and there's not much can go wrong. However, it is not that easy anymore because we have decided to take another route without taking God along with us. He is silent and we start to realize that we really miss the communication. We are losing sleep. We want an answer to the question of what to do now.

For whatever reason we can't seem to do what God says the first time. That would be too much like right. We'd rather take uncomfortable risks and make decisions on our on like we really know what's best and God is just so dumb. We forget all the mess we created before God went silent on us. He had been doing everything He knew to get our attention without yelling in our face. He just wants our time and effort, and to show Him that we are grateful for everything He has done for us. Notice that He is not looking for us to be blessed and boast and bring the next one down like we are so perfect. We become too stuck in our own talents and abilities and stop recognizing God's grace and mercy. We take God for a fool and come to Him only on occasions, giving Him false promises and proclaiming his name in vain.

It's just like us to want to make excuses for our actions. We will beat around every bush to hide the truth. We will disappear. We will laugh. We will be smiling in everyone's face though we know God is not pleased. We can't hide from God. We can't keep trying to play God for a fool, as if He knows nothing about us. God knows our thoughts before we think them. He knows our choices before we make them. God knows our strengths and weakness because He created us from head to toe. We can run but eventually God will get tired of us running, trying to hide from Him and everyone else. With love He will bring things to light so in the process He can break us down. He wants total honesty in everything we do even when we mess up.

I sometimes wonder how God's face changes when I do wrong, because it's something about the reaction I got from my mom when she knew I knew better. I could hear God calling my name, telling me to come and listening, but I ran and ran until I was forced to listen. I had been calling on God but He wasn't answering. He was waiting on me to get my stuff and mess together. He knew how much it would take for me to drop everything - I had to follow His will and His plan. It came as an unexpected surprise but I knew still who I could call on.

David found himself in the wilderness, calling on the name of God and asking how long, because God wouldn't answer him. I felt the same and perhaps you have too. We think God has forgotten us. We think He is going to let us drown in our own tears, but we haven't realized that for all the times we have forgotten God, He never forgets us. We are just too busy painting pictures and dreaming in a fantasy world, that we can't see the signs of danger that is telling us to chart a different course.

We see what we want to see. We tell God we are fed up with being misused, betrayed, judged by society, and being miserable altogether. Yet, we are running too fast, going at a swift pace, when God's time is not even a race. We are scared we are going to look bad if our sheet is uncovered. We are scared no one is going to call on us anymore, or be our friend. We are scared we're losing our minds and our hearts are being ripped out. But it's because we are living and dreaming in a fantasy world. The devil may have told you it was going to be easy, just go ahead and get on with it. He might tell you that it's going to get better, to just try it again and again. He is feeding your mind with poison and God is allowing you to experience the effects of following the wrong path.

David got to a point where he was wrestling with his own thoughts. Notice, it was with *his* thoughts. Thoughts that we create when we are hurt and in pain. We create thoughts that smooth over our wrongdoing. We create thoughts to blame others for our mistakes, even God. We create false assumptions of people that have done nothing but love and care for us. We stop looking at the big picture and start looking at the surface, not the root of our problem. And most times, the root is our own selfish motives. We could care less about what others have to say. We see great relationships broken because of our own thoughts being pushed back and forth by the devil himself. And sometimes we give in and conclude by affirming the devil. "It's not my fault - if you didn't do this then I wouldn't have done that."

We tend to forget that we are in control of our actions. No one can control what we say or do. Our thoughts leave us in more pain because we constantly dwell on the past and do not learn how to move forward. We get off track, and it gets a little fuzzy, so we end up running into things without seeing why. David knew why, because he chose his own way even after God had blessed him so many times before. He had an inflated head that was hung low when he saw that everything that he thought was good for him turned out to be very sour. The sourpatch candy sales pitch, incidentally, claims that their candy is first sour then sweet.

Our lives are always going to stay sour if we let the devil or our plans come before the Lord. If we let our thought alone control our actions, nothing good will come of it. David knew he was wrong, that's why he wrestled with his own self. And sometimes we know we are wrong and we wrestle with ourselves.

David goes on to ask God how long his heart will be in sorrow, thinking that his enemy will triumph over him. That makes me think back to scripture where it says, *weeping may endure for a night but joy cometh in the morning light.* I know David probably couldn't see at first any joy coming from his hurt and his sorrow. He mostly likely did what some of us do - we replay the bad and we try to pinpoint the enemy who has caused all our pain. We try to search every action and reaction of those we really care about. We go as far as we can in the past to see just what happened and why we are in this place.

I have come to tell you that sometimes the enemy is not the devil, but rather ourselves. We place ourselves in avoidable situations time after time. We have to cry, then blinded through the sorrow in our heart, we feel we are victims while everyone else is the suspect. We can't see wrong in ourselves, but in everyone else. We need to start sweeping around our own body, our own house and our own temple, before we can tell someone else how they should live and be. We must stop worrying about everyone else and get our own mess together. We all need to clean what we messed up and start all over again. This is the path towards the Christian example.

What do we do when it seems like God is not there? When it seems like God has closed up shop and isn't coming to answer the door, especially when we need him the most? Lament is the word you use to describe what you feel like when you are slowly disintegrating and your world is falling in on you, and all you can do is cry out to God, and ask how long? How long must this go on?

There are three things that bring David to lament in this psalm. We are forced to be honest with God when we can't find Him, when all we can do is cry and reach for Him, even when we feel it to be harder and harder to trust Him with the situation we are in.

We have to remember that in the weakest times and points, God is still in control and is still our strength. Notice that David doesn't call on just any god, he calls on 'My God,' which means he is calling on the one he knows is the real deal. The one to answer his prayers. While he can't figure out what God is doing, he knows that nevertheless God is the one and only place he must go to find support. When we can't hear or see God, we have one powerful weapon and that is prayer. God will not allow His children to be defeated because prayer shows him how faithful and trusting we are of Him when we have to turn our back on everyone and everything. Our praying life must increase day after day. He is tired of us talking to everything and everyone else but refuse to talk to Him. We refuse to let go and give it all over to Him.

He breaks us down to see what we couldn't see before. There are no clear answers, at least not immediately. That's why some of us go through certain types of physical suffering, financial hardship, relationship heartbreak, or emotional pain. But our lament, as we experience these things, can still find a true and powerful resolution once we realize the powerful answer God has in fact given us. This answer is Himself, and even more a relationship with Him where we can see and know Him for who he really is.

Trust comes not so much from looking at your present circumstances but at the past. And what the past reveals is who God really is - namely, a God who is always loyal and committed to those with whom He is in a relationship. To enter into a relationship with God is to enter into a commitment that God will never abandon. Consider the words of Jesus on the cross, "My God, my God, why have you forsaken me?" That is the cry of lament. This is the cry of someone who knows what it is to feel abandoned, alone, and defeated. In Jesus what we are seeing is the Lord God allowing Himself to be forsaken, to go through the dark night like we all must do, so that He might establish a safe path through that night. By following Jesus, we can ourselves take that path and find a God in the end that we can trust and rejoice in.

David declared "Look on me and answer, LORD my God. Give light to my eyes, or I will sleep in death" (Psalms 13:3). I believe David at this point. David was so angry at God and his present situation that he tried to place himself over God. David begins to demand of God what he wanted God to do and how he wanted him to do it. David even goes as far as threatening his own life if God doesn't indeed place favor on him and bless him soon. David, like us, knew he had a purpose in life and knew that he needed to fulfill it. However, at this point his mind became so cloudy and destroyed that he didn't care if he lived or died.

In certain situations in life we become just like David, and get so caught up in the situation and the weakness that our faith has become. We become so weak we demand of our God to do as we say. Think about it - how foolish is it when a man tries to demand God to do something, when God is the creator of everything and has the power to strip us of everything at a drop of a dime?

Instead of dwelling on the good things God has already done for us, we blame Him for our own unhappiness. We blame Him for the setbacks and disappointments. We move from crying out to God to anger, demanding God's presence right then and there. It's a scary feeling when you can see yourself falling into a black hole and know its infinite depth, because every day you wake up you see nothing but darkness and a living nightmare. Our dreams that were once beautiful, even in reality, become a greater nightmare in our fantasy world. We lose control and go spiritually insane.

We always say after God has blessed us - that if it wasn't for Him, we don't know where we would be. Well, why do we constantly doubt God in the thick of the storm? We have seen rain before and we have seen it disappear, right? That means rain and storms are only temporary. Yes, they can come and sweep everything from us. Our houses, our pride, even at times, our most prized possessions - what we forget to realize is that God is still in control.

He can tell the storm to cease whenever He is ready. He can call the winds to calm down. Let me tell you, there is nothing that is too hard for God. God has it all in control and He puts that reassurance deep in our soul for a reason.

When you look back on your life you should realize that you are only where you are now because, even when you couldn't see and weren't in control, God grabbed you and your situation and claimed victory for you. The devil has taken his best shot with you for long enough. The devil knows that God has the power to change the situation at a drop of a dime - which we *must* have faith and call on God.

We have to be willing to trust Him no matter what is going on. Let Him take the remote in our lives and change the channel from that scary picture to a sunny movie. Let Him hold your hand and guide you to the light. Aren't you tired of crying tears and turning around in circles? Can you finally see the sign that says *to turn around*, that you are going the wrong way? Can you hear God, and even when you don't, can you praise Him from the depths of your soul?

God has to destroy our ego and pride before He can use us, because He wants the glory of our life, and not see us continue to give the praise to the devil who has been infecting us.

God is tired of excuses. He is asking how long will you reject His calling on your life. How long will you let the devil defeat you when He called you to victory? How long will you keep trying to play saved? How long will you destroy your temple, which is your body? How long will you curse Him and act like it never occurred? How long will you deny his Word and His way? How long will you try to make Him out to be a fool? God has been trying to find out how long we will keep going in the wrong direction.

Does He have to kill us spiritually before we understand? Does He have to strip us of everything before we call on His name? How long before we realize we can't move or have our full being without Him? How long will we worship idols and false gods, and give everyone else more time and effort then we give Him? How long will we rob His temple with our tithing and turn around and ask for an increase? How long will we fight with Him instead of giving Him our all and moving forward with life? How long will we blame everyone else for our mistakes and our own choices in life? How long will we be disobedient to our elders and parents? How long will we disrespect his children, whether black or white, poor or rich? How long will we hold our head up high as we watch our brothers' and sisters' heads hang lower than before?

We have demanded, based on our wants and needs, so long that we have ignored what God wants and needs from us. We are too busy trying to be blessed that we can't be a blessing. We are demanding things out of selfishness and arrogance, and God is not pleased at all. He is doing everything to get our attention, with all manner of disasters. He is trying tell us to get it right, in a hurry, because we need a new beginning. God has done so much for us, so why can't we see that He is going do it again and again, that He is going to pick us up even at our lowest point? He will remove every enemy and not let them touch us, because we must believe in our own deliverance and restoration. We must increase our faith in bad times and not decrease it, because we can't see the end result. We must trust God beyond what we can see and walk on, standing firm and strong even if we have to stand alone. God is able to carry your load, and He can see way down the road before you even reach your destination. Let Him be your motivation every day at work and at home.

The next time, instead of demanding that God answer prayers for strength and guidance, just trust Him through it all. There is a song that says *never would have made it* by a gospel Artist named Marvin Sapp. This was an ordinary man after God's own Heart that understood that through everything he had been through, it was God that brought him out and through. It goes on to say *I'm stronger, I'm wiser and I'm better*. Marvin Sapp is just a brief example of how holding on to faith and trusting God looks in the end. He is a well- known gospel artist, who ministers all over the world. It was not overnight. However. It was a process that got him to that point. It was a constant faith walk with God.

This means that you should trust in Him. God told me to tell you to stop trying to figure it out. He has it all under control. Leave it alone! Stop crying, stop blaming yourself and others. You have no business doubting the Lord when you know He is that which can do above and beyond all that we have asked of Him. Stop getting angry when others you see are being blessed. Your time is coming - you just have to be patient, wait on Him, and keep moving forward. It's okay to look back, but do not dwell on the past. Realize who has held your hand time after time. When everyone else cut the strings and let you down to fall hard, God was there to pick you up and make you stronger than you have ever been.

The peace you are looking for can only be given by God. That man you want to love, only God can give you him. That relationship that is broken with your loved one, only God can mend it. God is the source of our strength and the strength of our life.

I encourage you today to leave your situation alone. Pray, thank God that He revealed the answer to you and move on. Stop making yourself, and everyone around you, miserable. People have enough problems of their own to deal with than to get lost in your issues. Sometimes we have to bear things without friends and family and just give in to God. We are so busy being judgmental and self-righteous that we can't seem to get our affairs right before God. Sometimes the enemy we fight is no one but ourselves.

If you don't want your own human nature and flesh to overtake you, get into the Word of God and ask God to help you overcome your situation. Stop looking for those miracles from humans, because they are not going to do anything but disappoint you more. They are going to smile in your face and stab you in the back. They are humans, made in God's image but cursed with sin. They make mistakes like you do. Carry your temptations, mistakes, struggles, and confusion to God. That's what God is saying to us right now - that there is nothing more that we can do but keep moving forward, stay on track and stand strong.

Don't make your situation a lot harder than it has to be. We will make ourselves sick while running around frantically trying to do everything without God by our side. God should be the first we come to in any situation. He shouldn't have to be the last.

God told me to tell you He is tired of being last. He is tired of coming second to the world. He is tired of us rethinking His love and power over our lives. He is tired of seeing us hurt when that is not what He wanted to happen. Just like when your parents called you to do something and you learned there was no way around it, God is saying the same thing. He doesn't care about our plans. Whatever He says needs to be done without complaint and hesitation.

Finally, David declared, "But I trust in your unfailing love; my heart rejoices in your salvation. I will sing the LORD's praise, for He has been good to me" (Psalm 13:6). David knew through it all that God wasn't the problem or blame. He was still there holding his hands like He did so many times before. He is still the same God, as in the last year, month, or even week, and He isn't going to change.

I thank God that when we start to doubt Him, He proves us wrong! He is going be firm and strict and whip us when need it. Though it makes us angry and hurt for the moment, we know it makes us stronger, wiser, and so much better.

God loves you and He wouldn't want to lose you - He will do what needs to be done to make sure that doesn't happen! Stop asking God how long and start asking Him for patience.

Put praise on your lips. Think about all the times you could have been dead and gone. He speaks when we don't expect Him to and He moves right when we are ready to give up.

Many times I shouldn't have made it in life but I'm a living witness that God is a God of grace and mercy. I dare you to give Him praise before you receive the breakthrough. Give Him a shout, even when you don't feel like talking. Be like David and think back to His unfailing love. Have enough faith to move forward. I promise God will handle the rest.

Many counted you out, but you are still here. Thank God for His covering of your life and that you didn't lose your mind when the devil attacked you over and over again. You are here for a purpose. You are a miracle and wonderfully made. Do not let the devil keep lying to you. Stop believing the enemy and believe God! Grab hold to God's love and forgiveness and walk by faith, not by sight. May God bless you and forever keep you covered and favored through His blessings.

He is ready to move now, but we have to be ready to move along with Him. We have to stop demanding what we want God to do, as if He is nothing to us but a servant. We are all called to be a servant of God, to bless Him. Don't you want to give Him control back, and stop feeling compelled to the world? If you are about ready to give up because you do not see results, keep holding on - God is still working it out! I want you to know you are getting ready to walk into a new season from deliverance to the healing you have been praying for! Watch God work it out for you!

Chapter 5

Free Me From All My Chains

Acts 12: 1 It was about this time that King Herod arrested some who belonged to the church, intending to persecute them. **2** He had James, the brother of John, put to death with the sword. **3** When he saw that this met with approval among the Jews, he proceeded to seize Peter also. This happened during the Festival of Unleavened Bread. **4** After arresting him, he put him in prison, handing him over to be guarded by four squads of four soldiers each. Herod intended to bring him out for public trial after the Passover. **5** So Peter was kept in prison, but the church was earnestly praying to God for him. **6** The night before Herod was to bring him to trial, Peter was sleeping between two soldiers, bound with two chains, and sentries stood guard at the entrance. **7** Suddenly an angel of the Lord appeared and a light shone in the cell. He struck Peter on the side and woke him up. "Quick, get up!" he said, and the chains fell off Peter's wrists. **8** Then the angel said to him, "Put on your clothes and sandals." And Peter did so. "Wrap your cloak around you and follow me," the angel told him. **9** Peter followed him out of the prison, but he had no idea that what the angel was doing was really happening;

he thought he was seeing a vision. **10** They passed the first and second guards and came to the Iron Gate leading to the city. It opened for them by itself, and they went through it. When they had walked the length of one street, suddenly the angel left him. **11** Then Peter came to himself and said, "Now I know without a doubt that the Lord has sent his angel and rescued me from Herod's clutches and from everything the Jewish people were hoping would happen." **12** When this had dawned on him, he went to the house of Mary the mother of John, also called Mark, where many people had gathered and were praying. **13** Peter knocked at the outer entrance, and a servant named Rhoda came to answer the door. **14** When she recognized Peter's voice, she was so overjoyed she ran back without opening it and exclaimed, "Peter is at the door!" **15** "You're out of your mind," they told her. When she kept insisting that it was so, they said, "It must be his angel." **16** But Peter kept on knocking, and when they opened the door and saw him, they were astonished. **17** Peter motioned with his hand for them to be quiet and described how the Lord had brought him out of prison. "Tell James and the other brothers and sisters about this," he said, and then he left for another place. **18** In the morning, there was no small commotion among the soldiers as to what had become of Peter. **19** After Herod had a thorough search made for him and did not find him, he cross-examined the guards and ordered that they be executed.

I praise God for the unanswered results! When I begin to look back, I can now praise God for the things that didn't happen, even when I prayed and wanted them to so badly! I had allowed myself to be fooled by the enemy and to be placed in past feelings of immobility. These reflections come from the following story.

I was recently engaged to a young man that convinced me he was ready to settle down and consider me alone as his wife. I think I was so distracted by the whole idea of being truly loved that I missed the signs of destruction telling me I was going in the wrong direction. I became bound by the fact he was the first guy that loved me and also broke my heart. However, I felt a need to begin again with him, hoping things would be different. I began to paint pretty pictures of him in my head, attempting to convince myself that he was the one for me. However, realities began to hit as I asked God to reveal secrets that I felt were hidden from me. God allowed me to see things I never want to see again.

Let me take you back to the day I thought this guy saved my life, and I thought I owed him mine. I was coming home with my friends. Midterms were over and I had a 4.0 GPA at the time. I was so excited and ready to tell my mom the good news, but in the excitement I ended up calling this guy, my first love, and someone that I hadn't been able to see in many years. He came and picked me up and he started to drive me home. He said we were five minutes away from my house. In those five minutes the unthinkable happened.

(September 16 2012 – Automobile wreck)

I fell asleep and woke up to yet another nightmare. I felt a rush of pain in my hip and saw nothing but darkness, and was seemingly in the middle of nowhere. I started to cry and scream because I didn't know what I was going to do. I had never been in a wreck before. I realized that I was in the wreck with the guy who made my heart race. I started praying. He got out of the car and ran to my side to get me out. We were stuck but I knew God was still there. I wanted to hear God, tell Him something, but all I could see was the crash in my head over and over again.

I was in shock, trying to put the pieces together on the spot - how this happened, why it happened. I ran to grab my phone to call my friends. I wished I'd stayed with them. They told me I needed to get home, and if they needed to, they would come to get me. I thanked them and I told the guy how desperately I needed to get home, given the amount of pain I was in. I called 911 and police and ambulance came. He had no insurance, so he told them I was fine and we would get home. I was terrified. He told me to call the towing company and pay to get his mother's truck back to Jackson.

Now let's stop and analyze this for a second, watching for the signs I missed. First, the guy was not worried at all about me, he was only concerned about the truck. He didn't pay to get me home but told me to pay to ride in a truck with a stranger instead of going straight to the hospital. If that wasn't enough, he also had the nerve to tell me not to call my godfather, but God spoke through me and said, "You must get out!"

I thought this meant from the house to the hospital, but I came to understand that it was from the relationship itself! My godfather came and took me to the hospital. At this point I was in so much pain that he called my mom, who didn't know I was in town trying to surprise her with my good news. She instead received a horrible call telling her that her daughter had been in a serious wreck.

After looking at the doctor's face, I knew it was nobody but God that intervened that day. God was telling me to stop and slow down because I was headed down a dangerous path and Satan just tried to take me out.

The doctor told me, "You shouldn't be alive. God must have

His hands on you."

All I could do was cry out to God. I was hurt, confused, and broken. In the few seconds that I thought was going the right way, I allowed Satan to imprison me and keep me bound to his will and his way. God allowed that wreck to wake me up; he allowed the path I thought I needed to travel to come to an end. He cleared my blinded eyes to see the trick of the enemy, to force me to slowly weave myself out of the devil's trap. It was hard, this process of praying, but when I freed myself from every hurt, memory, experience, and word that destroyed my heart - all my chains were broken. I received the key, which was God.

I was so weighed down by my baggage and so distracted by the enemy that I took my eyes off God. It wasn't a mistake, but it was the shaking and beating that prepared me to be God's vessel. I realized I no longer needed to follow my way and will, but God's way and will. He could have taken me that day, but He chose to let the enemy see that he couldn't kill what God had anointed to live. Because of God I had no broken bones, had no screws installed, and I did not need surgery. All I needed was a word and direction from God!

I just thank God he prevented the greater destruction before I saw it coming. I was giving in and settling for less than what God had intended for me. God told me He had too much in store for me to allow me to settle for anything. He said He was the key to breaking through. I thought God wasn't there when the whole time I wasn't paying attention; I was looking at the surface and focusing more on the devil's tricks than God's power to free me from my accumulated life's baggage.

Sometimes you may be ready to give in, because it seems like all has failed when you reach out for help, but your trust in Him is never in vain. Please get ready for Him because you are on the rise! Satan is not the key, but instead he can bind you in all kinds of ways. Let God deliver, restore, and establish you all over again. I asked God to make me over and he did. He will do the same for you.

Have you ever felt so bound that you thought you would never break free and the enemy was winning? You felt like God was there, but you didn't know exactly when He would show up. Was He going to show up too late? Was He going to skip over your problems and issues in life or was He too busy to handle the very thing you had been crying out to Him about?

You sometimes believe in the promise of His Word again, but you may not be sure if God is going to come to your rescue on time. You've prayed and maybe even tried fasting, but after all that, life's bills are still piling up. Your house is still almost up for foreclosure, and your friends are still few. You can't seem to get rid of that addiction, and you don't know if that bitter taste in your mouth and life will ever go away. You look around, and it seems like God has passed you by to rescue another. You tell yourself this battle is just too big, and the weight of life's baggage is too heavy. You don't know exactly when you are going to fall apart, but you seem to be getting closer to the edge. You look at the ground beneath you and you feel stuck in your own mess.

You begin to wonder when you are going to be able to move forward. God has talked to you over and over again, but you haven't seen the results you were looking for. You want to know that your faith is not in vain. You want to know that all that crying out to God wasn't a waste of time.

You don't want to look like a fool for preaching and encouraging when your life is just too much of a mess. It may seem like your best is just not good enough. You may have even decided to give it all over to God, but have grown a little impatient. You have received the answer you have been searching for, yet you still don't have any results to draw from it. You finally have found just a little bit of peace in your life. But every time you look around that same thing, that gnawing set of memories and patterns, creeps up and it changes your mood or day. It takes you back to a place you never wanted to see again. It binds you from moving where God is trying to take you. You are so stuck that you don't think your chains can get any tighter.

I want you to know you are not alone. Though you cannot see the results right now, if you trust in God, the almighty King, you can break free from everything that has you bound.

In life, at times, we have to go through a "prisoner stage." You may have heard the saying, "If you don't do the crime you can't do the time." Well, that still stands firm in the Christian faith and life. We must not keep thinking we can keep putting God on the back burner of our lives, which is our Christian crime. For that crime, we are doing the time, not living whole lives. That goes as far as He commands His will for our lives. God is not pleased with us giving everything glory and praise except Him. Have you noticed that everything now is about entertainment instead of true ministry? The enemy has taken our sense of true worship and anointing away. This is a drift towards a crime of glorifying the earthly at the expense of the divine.

There is nothing wrong with fast-paced songs and the gospel music. My concern is are we truly receiving God's presence or is that our high for the hour, then we go home and continue the way things were? It takes *true* worship and praise to enter into the presence of God. The choir is a wonderful addition to usher the spirit, but it acts as a supplement for entertainment, even in the choir stand. We cannot continue the way things are. It is time for a real breakthrough in our church houses as well as our own lives.

As Christians, we feel compelled to conform to the way of the world because we want to be accepted into a decadent society, or we want to shine in the spotlight like so many in power. We are missing the main ingredient in this relationship we are building with God, and that is total commitment. This relationship we have with God must be constant and not just a fleeting fling. How would you appreciate it if God decided He was going to claim you only when it was convenient for Him?

I would hate to hear God sell me out because I didn't do what He wanted right away, as much as I appreciate the wisdom of his tests. Thankfully, God is the opposite of selfish, greedy, or demanding in this relationship He has built with all believers. He is a loving and forgiving, most unselfish thing you will ever come in contact with.

God gives each of us a choice. He does not force us to love Him. He does not seek revenge when He is hurt, and He never brings up the past. God gives us second chance after second chance. Let me ask you, how many chances has God given you? How many times did you really disappoint God?

We constantly crawl in the Christian faith, but won't start walking. When a baby crawls, it begins on what you could call beginner's luck. You may be wondering how a baby crawling would be considered as luck? As an infant, the baby only receives certain things at certain times. The mother has a set naptime, set feeding times, and she keeps certain things out of reach from the baby until they begin to walk and when she feels they are ready. When the baby learns to crawl, it discovers a different world. The baby begins to observe things for what they are. It sees and knows what has been held back from him or her, not because they didn't deserve it, but because they weren't ready. The baby might want to be fed but the mom tells them, "It's not time yet," but the baby proceeds to crawl toward the bottle anyway. The baby can either wait on the mother's time to receive the bottle that they just can't seem to live without, or they can crawl their way to the bottle that's out of reach. Maybe the bottle might just fall within reach.

To those who may have just missed this—when we first started the Christian journey, we were all at a crawling stage. God knew when we needed to be blessed and how to bless us. In certain times in our lives, God had to keep some things out of our reach. He knows what is best for us when we don't know how the devil is working. God doesn't keep our blessings out of reach because we don't deserve them. Like that mother to her child, He knows when we are ready to handle the blessing and when we are not ready to handle it. We were not prepared for his ultimate purpose and plan for our lives.

We have taught ourselves how to crawl - how to read His Word and how to pray when we need Him the most. We are like that baby who wants and needs something that God is just not ready for us to have. That could be money, a spouse, or even a career, but since we have learned to crawl and get through some tunnels, we feel entitled to whatever it is that we want. We begin to go through life thinking on those terms. Yet, knocking down everyone else in our pursuits will put us in reach of the very thing God is not ready for us to have.

Think of the lottery. We know God owns everything, but in the moment of trouble we tend to not want to walk in faith and trust God, but crawl and lean toward the devil's temptations and plans. I always wondered why certain things always happen to good people; and now, after learning how to walk in my faith, to stop crawling and trying to force shortcuts to God's blessings, I'm wondering why we constantly deny God to the unbelievers when he has been so good to us.

If at this moment someone told you that you would lose everything you had if you were a believer in Christ, would you deny Christ? Your response probably would be an adamant, "No, I love God, and He is number one in my life." But when you hear God's voice and ignore it, you are denying Christ. When you hear your brother or sister is in trouble and you do nothing but gossip, you are denying Christ. When you hold grudges in your heart and mind, you are denying Christ. When you put everything before God, you are denying Christ. When you walk out of church because the preacher is not entertaining anymore or because it's not the word you want to hear, you are denying Christ. In other words, we are quick to say what we won't do as Christians because we supposedly love God so much, when in reality we are nothing but hypocrites who have denied Christ over and over again. I have come to tell you that God is not pleased with us only claiming Him when we need His help.

I know you get tired of those same people in your life that claim they love you, but only call you when they need or want something. You only hear from them every blue moon, when it suits them. Is that a true committed relationship? No, not at all. God is the same way - He is tired of us taking advantage of his anointing, blessings, and forgiveness. Too many times, with the blessings we receive from God, we start to boost ourselves up instead of thanking God. When God forgives us time and time again we conclude that we can do whatever we like with our lives, because God is a forgiving God. We feel we are going straight to heaven regardless because of simple understandings of Christian practice. We don't worship or praise God for His many blessings anymore; we just claim them and give God a little whisper of thanks and proceed to go about our lives like He has done nothing to make them possible.

We have become like robots marching for the devil and his society. We would rather program ourselves and our lives to please and be committed to money, power, and fame, rather than God's purpose and will for our lives. The devil has told us that tradition is the way to go, to never break from our routine. Because we like the comfortable way, instead of changing, we stay right where the devil knows how to attack us time after time.

Think about it. If in a sport the team never switches up the routine of their game, plays the same way every time, the opponents would know how to target them and ultimately be able to consistently defeat them. The devil has learned the way we live, who we live with, and when and where we go. He follows us around, waiting for us on that next trip, relationship, or job opportunity. His plans seek to destroy anything God has planned for our lives.

The enemy has replaced our common sense and knowledge of Christ with lies, throwing false prophets in our path, sending the wrong guy or girl that comes only to use us, sending a jealous coworker that's waiting for us to mess up so they can snatch our job and career. We have become chained in society, feeling like we are the only ones listening to God and hearing him speak. We begin to feel like misfits, but instead of walking in faith, we sell God out for our devilish thoughts and actions over and over again.

We are left wondering why we can't see the results of God's answer. Well, until you truly break free from the devil's plans and make a change, you will not see God working miracles in the midst of your mess. You will continue to feel stuck, bound by your past and your painful experiences. You will not be able to open your eyes to the change that could already be beginning to transform your life. Those chains will get tighter and tighter as long as we allow the devil to be king.

We must recognize that we are not prisoners in this world, but we are created by God himself. He is our King. He is the key to finding the peace we need to move forward, right to our full salvation.

How maddening is it when you cannot find peace? You are a Christian, right? But have you actually fulfilled your side of that relationship? You're supposed to be meditating on the Word day and night. God's Word is the Christian's sword. It is the key to breaking free from the chains of life. The sword breaks loose even those that feel their hope is gone and the enemy has guards all over, from front to back.

It seems like there is a wall blocking you from moving forward, right? But have you learned about Jericho? "By faith the walls of Jericho fell down after being encircled by the Israelites for seven days" (Hebrews 11:30). Joshua didn't have to fight the wall and the blockage it had imposed on everyone's life. He merely used God's spoken word, walked by faith around the wall, which then came tumbling down. We think the only way to get out of bondage is by crawling or fighting everyone and everything that's in our path. I don't know why we feel our attacks on others, heavy with false promises and spoken words, will raise us higher.

We have somehow crawled so much in life that we are now lost, and we have crawled into a state that leaves us unsure of which way to turn. We know the word and know how to pray, but why are we struggling to walk in faith? Why is it so hard for us to see now? Why are we looking only to go to church for our next high and not the Word of God?

God has given us the answer. The reason we fear the word is because the devil knows it is what will deliver us. He knows when God speaks into our heart there is nothing he can do to fight it. You think the devil wants you to worship God? Do you think he wants you to move all distractions and be touched by an angel of God to break free? No ma'am, no sir. The devil wants you to simply hear the beats to the new songs, not the lyric that was meant to speak to your soul. The devil doesn't want you to fill your life with positive people, because he knows wherever there is something positive God is also dwelling. The devil doesn't want you to succeed in life because he wants you to become imprisoned in his way of life. Since he has nothing going for him besides his life in Hell, he wants you to join him there.

My best friend would always tell me that misery loves company, and I've found that to be true in the Christian life. The devil doesn't like that he has messed up his own eternal life and can no longer feel God's presence like we can. He is jealous of how quickly God comes to our rescue even when we don't deserve it. The devil knows that we already have victory, so he is just wailing on the weak to make them a prisoner to his own misery. God's Word states, "For sin will have no dominion over you, since you are not under law but under grace" (Romans 6:14).

Looking at the sacred text, which is Acts 12, you see here that the king, who has all power, has called to place a believer into prison, which here is Peter. Now first, let me tell you a little about this true servant of God. So firm was Peter's faith that Jesus gave him the name of Cephas, meaning, in the Syriac language, "rock." It was Peter who preached to the masses in Jerusalem on the day of Pentecost. His message is recorded in the New Testament of the Bible, the Book of Acts. Peter is also the one who prompted the disciples to choose a replacement to take over the apostolic ministry of Judas Iscariot after Judas' betrayal of Jesus. It was Peter who healed a man, over 40 years of age and crippled from birth, with only the words, "Silver and gold I do not have, but what I have I give to you. In the name of Jesus Christ of Nazareth, walk." Peter was called by the apostle Paul a "pillar" of the Church. It was believed by the crowds that the mere casting of his shadow upon the sick was capable of bringing about miraculous healing. Peter is the one who defended the inclusion of the Gentiles into the Christian Church at the Apostolic Council in Jerusalem.

Peter sounds like a saint, right? Well, he continued to walk in faith and acknowledge Christ wherever he went. He did not care about what the unbelievers thought of him as long as God was pleased with him. I'm sure there were moments in his life where he felt like a misfit spreading the Word of God, but many denied. However, he didn't deny God - he kept putting God first and stomping on the devil when he appeared. He knew who had everything in control, no matter what situation he was placed into. You can see that in the text God allowed this wonderful servant to be placed in the hands of the devil for a while, just to see how real his faith was.

The king called four guards to watch Peter's every move. The king couldn't stand anyone overstepping his authority, and Peter was the misfit that refused to conform to the king's ways. Everyone else chose to bow down to the king's every word and deed, but Peter was that one who said, "No, I'm not going to please you and deny my father, my true king." Peter made up in his mind that he was ready to go into bondage for the services he was performing in the name of God. Peter didn't deny God and tore his knees crawling his way out of prison. He faced his time and punishment boldly while walking in nothing but faith. Peter didn't doubt God even when he couldn't see any results. He didn't go crying and hiding because things got tough.

Imagine, this man loves God, does everything he thought would please God, and yet is in chains on every side. There are guards in every corner and he feels the chains probably can't get any tighter at this point in life. But did Peter curse God's existence? Did he regret all he had done in God's name? No. Peter embraced the situation and trusted God that much more, called on God that much more, prayed that much more. In the thick of the storm, bound by the devil himself, Peter was touched by an angel in the middle of the night. The angel told him to put on his clothes and follow him. Peter didn't fear the angel, or the consequences of the king, but boldly took the cross with him and walked in faith, putting on the whole armor of God, breaking free from every chain that the devil thought he would never find the key for.

Some of you, like Peter, have been seen as true men of God, but when things are going poorly, you feel God is angry with you. I have come to tell you that is not the case at all. God is testing your commitment in your relationship with Him. He wants you to know now that He is strong enough to handle, not only the chains of your own life, but also those of others. He wants us all to be like Peter, to not doubt or deny Him in times of crisis. He wants to know that we will not continue to sell Him out to the enemy, as if He was a fleeting emotion and not the Lord.

We cannot keep treating God like a fling or fix for our own selfish pleasures. The devil may have called you to prison in your own life, to be chained and controlled by him. I have come to let you know that God is the key to breaking free. There is an angel that is tugging at your side, telling you not to give up or curse God, but put on His whole armor and walk in faith. This is the key to ultimate freedom in life. Faith is when we cannot see the results, but we still believe in the Word and walk boldly, servicing God and His people, not regretting our service but rejoicing in God in our every move.

Remember when Peter began to proclaim to everyone that he was free, and they thought he was talking foolishness, that he was a ghost, already dead and destroyed by the devil (through the king)? There are going be people in your life that don't believe that you have been set free, nor seen God's angels. These are the people that will test your faith and make you want to turn back into those same chains. Do not submit. God is the key to breaking free. Once He breaks you free, you mustn't let the devil lure you back into his traps. The way the devil tries to get to us is often through the people we know best. He knows that they have seen you hurt, weak, and down.He knows they have already probably counted you out, even when you don't even know it yet. Hold on to God and stay committed to Him. You do not have to conform to this world. Those very ones that have counted you out will begin to see God alive in you. They will see the change that has taken and is taking place.

Walk in faith and do not look back. The past will only drag you back in its wake. The past is full of the tests and trials you have already overcome. If you are called and anointed by God, do not be an uncomfortable misfit. Embrace the calling and gift that God decided to bless you with. Do not deny God's Word like you don't know it, when it is there to be had. Teach others what God has taught you through experience. Don't be afraid to speak boldly in the name of Jesus. Stand on God's Word.

Remember to paraphrase Jesus' words – "If you should be ashamed of me, I'll be ashamed of you in front of my Father" (Luke 9:26). Do you want Jesus to be ashamed of you in front of God? Do you want God to regret He gave you the anointing and the Holy Spirit on the Day of Judgment? You are not here to please people, nor the devil, so why would you be afraid to walk in faith? Why do you hesitate to send the Word forth when God commands and gives it to you?

Yes, it isn't an easy road when people aren't familiar with seeing you strong and full of the Holy Spirit. They might even think you have a way with words, that you're spinning a web. You have to declare defiantly that you are a child of God, and that you were chosen to be a servant and spread His Word. He sent an angel to touch you when you were surrounded by guards and chains. Once He saved you and set you free, He gave you commands to be followed. God's Word doesn't need an explanation.

When the preacher preaches, it's not always what we want to hear or how we want to hear it, but it is sent by God. No matter how it is sent or whom it is delivered through, the Word will always stand alone. It never loses its power. God has a greater plan for your life. He is not going to let you go through it blind. He is preparing you for the blessing that is ahead. Maybe you had it right at your fingertips the last time, but got off track and God sent you all the way back around to try again. It is fine to fail and mess up sometimes. We must all grow and learn from our mistakes. If we were perfect, we wouldn't need God. I need God more than anything; therefore I'm nowhere near prefect. I am a sinner trying to serve the Lord, to obey His will and way.

God is using young people because they aren't set in their ways - they are still learning, making mistakes, crying, and running from Him. He also knows we are the most honest and direct age group. We are not afraid of what people think of us. We aren't conforming to teachings of the day, because we are like new creatures who are trying to discover God and the world for ourselves. We are challenging what our parents were taught, not because we are disobedient, but because we are a new generation that seeks confirmation and adventure. That might be a well-worn way to live, but the end of our adventure is exactly where God meets us. There are countless powerful, anointed youth pastors, ministers, and even motivational speakers. However, some of us are so stuck in the past and blind, we can't see God using us to turn this world around, and helping everyone break free.

We have been brainwashed by false prophets that interpreted the Word the way they wanted. Many in the past have been based on what they speak only, speaking life into a group on false premises. "Beware of the false prophets, who come to you in sheep's clothing, but inwardly are ravenous wolves. You will know them by their fruits. Grapes are not gathered from thorn bushes, nor figs from thistles, are they" (Matthew 7:15)? We have to realize we are all fighting to get to Heaven, and segregating ourselves on those terms is to the detriment of us all.

Our generation comes with so much diversity, operating in ways that are distinguishing us from old ways of life. Our generation is seen as a misfit to all the rest, but God is still in control. He knows what He is doing and has impeccable timing. He knows we are not afraid to speak on His behalf.

Our problem is we are looking to be entertained; we want to see miracles in the flesh, not the spirit. We have to hear our pastor whoop and holler before we get the message. God will not scream at us. He will not force His attention on us. God comes in whispers. You must seek Him to have Him revealed. Our generation is not looking for old remedies to attend to our problems anymore. We are not seeking man's advice, we are seeking the truth. We are denying the religion and its outdated beliefs, and listening to what God tells us. It is not easy being denied by an older minister or pastor that was once right where we are. We need to push harder to establish our truth in God.

We too are tired of the way things are. We are asking God the questions many were too afraid to seek answers for. God is now putting us through things we shouldn't have to go through until an older age. God's timing is not always our timing. We wonder why the youth aren't in church. God told me that the church has become the new street. God is saying the church is no longer a holy place of worship, but we have allowed it to be a place of judgment, hypocrisy, and quick fixes. The church is no longer seen as a place to meet God. God has left the building.

In the book of Acts 6:18, it says, "In the morning, there was no small commotion among the soldiers as to what had become of Peter. After Herod had a thorough search made for him and did not find him, he cross-examined the guards and ordered that they be executed." After the storm and rain has passed over, when God moves on your behalf, there is nothing more the devil can do to you. Those people that talked you down and tried to destroy your dreams and callings will eventually be silenced, and will face judgment for their attempts on your holy life. You will have been moved past your hurdles in life, and will go about living.

I honestly can say I know God for myself. It is the best feeling and experience anyone can have. Whatever you need right now, ask God for it and be in a position to receive it. Stop robbing God. Stop treating Him like He means nothing.

Satan took your strength away, but God is ready to give you His power! We have to realize that God has the final Word and you are the chosen one! God is ready for you to turn your life back over to Him, and He will show you just real He is. We all have sinned and come short of the glory of God, but God wants you to know He will meet you right where you are, and can restore everything if you allow Him. Use the testimonies I have revealed from my life as an example of how powerful and good God can be. In the thick of a great mess, He can turn things around.

He is ready to restore your mind. He knows what you are going through and what you have been through. He knows you, and his relationship can only grow stronger if you do not stray from Him. Do not give the devil control over your life. Stop crying tears and start living in God. I thank God for the honor of speaking to you. I am ready to go forth in the calling as a true messenger from God. It's time to stop these games we play with ourselves and our communities. Like singer and actress Tamela Mann said, "We need a word for the people's pain. It's no longer about what we don't know but it's about what God is trying to let us know."

Give everything to Him. Learn to read and walk not by sight, but by faith. I have no doubt that you are going to make it to a place of divine joy. Mistakes will occur, but you must keep pushing, for God cares so much for you. He didn't bring you this far in life to just walk away and leave you – show the same commitment to Him. May God bless you and forever keep you.

That baggage you are constantly carrying around allows you to stay with your routines. Let go and walk, not through faith in the devil's works, but the faith in God's almighty power. You have to stop listening to everyone else and listen to God. Aren't you tired of going in circles? Don't you want to see a change take place?

It's time for you to stop placing demands on God. It's time to enter into true worship again! The reason you can't worship is because you are too distracted by the demons among us, by your own lack of submission of His will. You are afraid of what someone else has to say about you, but what is God saying? Ask yourself if God is pleased with your life and the time and effort you've given Him.

Chapter 6

Learning to Love Myself

When I used to hear the word "love" I heard the word "pain." Pain became like a scar or tattoo that was planted on my heart. It wasn't easy to remove. Have you ever gotten a tattoo that you felt you were going to love, but found yourself only tolerating it just because it was there? I felt like at birth I was tattooed with the sign, "Use and abuse me much as you please."

Most children from birth grow up with a loving family and a support system that can't be replaced. However, the kind of love I received as a child caused me to stop loving myself. I was one of the few that didn't understand the true meaning of the word love. I thought it was the constant beatings and bruises. I thought it was the screaming and yelling, the negative cursing on my life. Like so many other children around the nation, when I used to hear the word love, I was confused about how to love and about who really loved me.

Growing up in a home where love was never really shown was like growing up in a wilderness where there was neither protection nor direction. I realized the love I knew wasn't love at all, because of this piece of scripture: "Love is patient and kind" (Corinthians 12:4-8). This changed my whole life forever. It taught me that love wasn't a convenient title to manipulate the one who poured their life, heart, or soul out to you. In other words, love wasn't a word to throw around because you felt you had to get what you wanted from someone.

How many times have you found yourself loving someone so intensely that you neglected to love yourself? I mean this is the sense of truly loving who you are, even your flaws. Many times in life, we see people lose themselves in the name of *love*.

Imagine this. It was on a Sunday morning and this young girl by the name of Maykaya was getting ready for church. She heard her name being screamed. "Maykaya! What are you doing?" She was very reluctant to examine the situation that was at hand, fearing she would only find a person that used the word love in public, while constantly shouting hate in her eyes.

To the scream, she would reply, "Cleaning my room" or "Getting dressed."

The voice would get louder. "Come eat!"

In her mind, at this point, she wanted to shout, "You eat the damn food!" She didn't have enough backbone at the time to stand up for herself. She slowly walked down the stairs, feeling like she was ready to vomit. She walked into the kitchen, to see that everything appeared the same. Except, there laid a plate of bacon, eggs, toast, biscuit, rice or oatmeal, depending on what one's tastes may have been that day. There was one table with a cup of water and orange juice on it. You would think Maykaya was about to have a huge feast – she was wrong.

"Sit down, you devil," her mom said.

Maykaya politely told her, "I'm not very hungry. I'm going to go back upstairs."

Her mom proceeded to lift her hand. *Bam! Bam!* Two slaps to the face, and Maykaya forcibly being pushed into the chair, was all it took.

Maykaya sat there for a minute, tears flowing down her face. In the back of her head, she wanted to run out the door and never come back. However, she sat upright, hoping she would calm her mom down. Her mom stood over her, waiting for her to pick up the fork for the first bite. As she was trying to compose herself, her hand started to shake badly.

Maykaya dared not tell her mother, again, that she wasn't very hungry. She took the biggest bite possible, hoping the food would somehow disappear, like some type of magic act.

Her mother standing over her shouted, "Eat faster!"

Maykaya started to force food down her throat, though every bite disgusted her. The faster she went, the quicker she would vomit it all up. Her mother seemed to love that part the best. Maykaya would begin to make gagging sounds to warn her mother that she couldn't eat any more. However, it only caused her more pain.

Her mother gave her an evil look and said, "Eat it all."

Her mother's face became more ghostly at that point. While forcing food down her throat, she was gagging at the same time. She didn't understand what was happening or why the person would intentionally fix enough food for a family of four, while it was only her at the table. After finally gagging enough to throw it all up, it all went flying out her mouth. This was the worst mistake she could have made.

The mother proceeded to raise her hand again. *Bam! Bam! Bam!* Yes, another three slaps to her face and head, knocking her to the floor, where her vomit had landed. She rushed to get herself up and clean everything, but it was too late. *Whap, whap, whap*, and a lot more hits came her way.

She yelled, "It hurts! It hurts!"

"It is supposed to hurt you!" her mother yelled back. "Now sit here. I can't get ready because you want to be the devil every Sunday morning."

Maykaya said, "I'm sorry. I didn't mean to be the devil." Her next instructions were to clean up the mess, and hurry before her mother left her alone at the house.

Maykaya is no longer being *loved* in that way. However at the time, she feared her mother and her voice so much that she did everything that pleased the mother, even when she was the one suffering. Yes, she did this in the name of love. Did that sound like love to you? I'm sure not, but it was the love she knew and began to tolerate. Each time it happened she told herself that love was pain, love was abuse.

I'm sure that scenario was shocking, but Maykaya lived it day in and day out. Though this may be very traumatic, for the reader it was reality. She found herself accepting violence against her because, like many victims of abuse, she told herself she deserved the hurt. She related to that woman or man that grew up having to smile to keep from crying and be silent in the name of love.

You may be asking, why I used Maykaya as an example. Maykaya represents the nation of abused women and men, who can't bear to reveal that they are mistreated and misused physically, mentally, and emotionally behind closed doors. You will notice that it is Maykaya's mother that is the abuser. I am sure this is someone that you would not imagine would be the suspect. However, many times we associate unconditional love with an image of a parent and their child, yet fail to realize the reality that not every mother is a nurturing one. Not every father is a provider, and not every child feels the warmth of love daily.

If you are one of those men or women that can relate to the pain and constant suffering of a dark secret that is happening or has happened behind closed doors, I want you to understand that the only solution is to forgive and move forward. The reason Maykaya is not loved in that manner anymore is not because she gave up on life and sought revenge, but she realized her true value. Maykaya learned to love herself and not allow her mother to destroy her.

You may be dealing with trauma from a spouse, parent, sibling, aunt, or uncle, but I want you to understand that you have value and are important. I can relate to the constant flashbacks, nightmares, and regrets of not fighting back from the abuse I encountered in the home I lived in.

Yes, I was just like Maykaya. I was filled with hatred and bitterness deep down in my heart, with every scar, and every slap or negative word that broke me down with each day that went by. I learned that the only way to free myself and learn to love who I am was to forgive the person that taught me that "love was pain and love was abuse." You cannot continue to let that person control, your mind, actions, and life anymore. I encourage you to fully free those chains over your heart, and let God restore you. I had to learn that forgiveness is not for them but it's for me.

Then Peter came and said to Him, "Lord, how often shall my brother sin against me and I forgive him? Up to seven times? Jesus said to him, "I do not say to you, up to seven times, but up to seventy times seven" (Matthew 18:21-22). It is not a certain number of times we are to forgive, but forgiveness has no limits. However, just because we forgive doesn't mean we remain in the same situation that God desires to truly deliver us from. "It was for freedom that Christ set us free; therefore keep standing firm and do not be subject again to a yoke of slavery" (Galatians 5:1).

There are countless women and men that do not understand the meaning of love because they have only felt pain where love might have been. We are afraid to face reality in life, because reality is a scary state of being. I cry out for that girl that's searching for love in all the wrong places. While searching for love, she may have had her heart broken by men and women. I emphasize the experiences of women. When a girl is raped by her father, she finds herself hating men and finds comfort in women. Likewise, when a man is touched inappropriately by his father or uncle at a young age, he becomes confused about his own identity. Instead of Christians embracing those confused women or men, they reject their experiences. All that is left for them is pain and a constant searching for that slippery concept of *true love*.

We are so quick to judge others that we forget the thorns in our sides. We go through life *drunk in love*. To be drunk means to not have a mind of our own, constantly poisoning our bodies in unthinkable ways. We find it pleasurable to be causing ourselves and others deep pain.

We will kill our family members' pride and ambitions in the name of this thing called love. I don't know why, but one of the most common abuser's excuse is "I'm doing this because I love you." They know the love felt (one way) towards them will only confuse the mind into accepting the pain, thinking it is a sign of being loved in return.

I cry out to that mother who is silently being abused sexually, emotionally, and physically, yet is expected to continue to smile, because she is married and has loving kids. I wonder how long society will help paint this deceiving picture of love. It leads me to the question, "How far, in the name of love, will we go before we say enough is enough? How many times do we have to be asked, "Are you okay?" before we drop our pride, and say, "No, I am miserable." We tend to hide our pain so far away that we forget how much we are really hurting ourselves.

Whenever I would find myself in a place of unbearable pain, the church became my place of peace. Not because of the people on the roll book, but because I knew I could be blessed in the name of God. I would go to church in so much pain, wanting to break out in tears, crawling my way to the altar, afraid and confused. I had been exposed to churches that waited for people to go to the altar, and in the name of love, acted as if they really cared about what they were going through, yet turned around and tore down the names of the broken ones at the altar. I thank God that not all churches are like this.

Like many young people in my generation, I was afraid to show my pain. Every Sunday, I only walked past the altar that I knew was a place of healing, and restoration, dying more and more inside.

How many times have you gone to church because it was a routine? When was the last time that you actually thirsted for God's embrace? I remember the times I went without being able to feel the presence of God. Yet, when I went home and studied the Word for myself, I felt God like never before. At this time, I didn't understand this concept because the church was, in my mind, the only place to experience God's love, grace, and mercy. However, I slowly found out that God's love didn't start in the church and surely wasn't going to end there. In other words, God helped me understand that though the altar was a known place for repentance and forgiveness, I could get that same experience anywhere on Earth.

After learning and understanding this, I noticed that church was not just a building to attend an uplifting ceremony, but to build a different relationship with God. This only happened when I took time out from my busy day to open my Bible and study for myself. Once I started to seek God for myself, I had no desire to worry about things I could not control. When I got to church, the preacher didn't have to hype me up for me to worship God. I didn't have to hear the shouting music to shout through my spirit. I didn't have to depend on someone speaking to me to keep a smile on my face. The church became a place where all I wanted to do was bless the name of God, a special place where God (who is everywhere) can be celebrated in the fullest.

I challenge anyone who is in a state of depression, sickness, or loneliness to start blessing the name of God. Blessing God doesn't mean to just grab everyone in reach and demand that they attend church, but committing one's self to the will and way of God. I know it gets hard sometimes, dealing with the flashbacks or the pain that haunts you. I learned through my storms, that sometimes God doesn't move exactly when expected, but always moves right on time. Yes, I got angry, and my patience wore thin. I realized no matter how much I cried or threw a fit, God, wouldn't move until He was ready. He wanted me to understand that I wasn't my own God, and He wasn't moved by my tears, but by praise alone.

To those of you that were and are like me, and can't see love because you experienced so much pain, I want to share with you that love is not pain at all. Love is the opposite of pain. Love is a sweet smell and taste, not a bitter one. Love is something that reflects someone who cherishes you for who you are, not for what you can do for them. Love is not a relation of abuse or neglect, but one of tender care.

If you are in a situation right now where you are suffering and neglecting to love yourself, God wanted me to let you know that now is the time to come out. Now is the time to take your life back and embrace the gift of love. God is love. He wants to show us that love doesn't have to hurt or feel like an everlasting curse.

I used to think that I wouldn't be loved by anyone because of the pain I kept sending myself back to. It took me letting go and forgiving anyone that caused me pain to experience the love that God wanted for me. God wants you and me to live a life of peace and happiness. He doesn't desire for us to constantly force ourselves to be in a relationship of any kind with someone that claims love is pain and love is abuse.

I'm a witness to the fact that love can be confusing, tormenting, and deceiving when it comes to loving the wrong things and people in life. I had to learn that love didn't come from smooth talking or dressing the part. Love was that unconditional substance that only God can give. This extends beyond sex as well. We, as humans, try to love but fall short every time, because we don't truly understand that love is not sex.

I remember crying out to God one night in my room trying to find out why every guy I cared for so much left me in tears and regret. I found myself wanting to give up my body for this thing called love. I was ready to convince myself that I would only find true love if I gave in to pressure and society's view on love, which so often is focused on sex. I want to let young men and women know that if he or she loves you, they will wait for you. Don't fall so hard in love that you can't think for yourself anymore.

As a young woman, I promise you that it is the best feeling in the world to know I have control over my own body. I don't have to think back and figure out why I have not let any given person be my first. I can say that though it has been hard holding on to my virginity, it is the best choice I could have made for myself.

I am not perfect, and yes, I too have hormones and desires, but I also have a future. Though I wanted to be popular and have pretty babies one day, I learned that life and love was much more than that. I used to get called every name in the book that degraded who I was, but I never allowed that to determine who I would become. I learned that sex is a beautiful gift from God, but only in its proper time. I used to hear that I was being selfish by not allowing a man to experience my body. I want anyone that is also dealing with this to know that men or women that force this question don't truly love you. No one that can boldly claim love for you will ever force you into an act that goes against everything you believe in and value.

Every action has a reaction. Just because in your past you experienced hate and pain doesn't mean that you should stop loving yourself. We can't truly experience the meaning of love until we learn to love who we are, who God created us to be. I learned very quickly that if I didn't love myself first, people were going to continue to treat me as if I wasn't meant to be loved. God wants you to understand that loving yourself and doing what is best for you right now is love. It is His will that you find the best choice you can make.

Chapter 7

Keep Your Focus

Many times in life, we are focused on the wrong things. Imagine trying to complete an assignment but every time you start your focus is pulled in another direction. The call that is on our lives is constantly being challenged. Not just by our struggles and mistakes along the way, but it is like a *game* of some sort. Why is it that many people achieve things at great heights while others only continue to dream and ponder about the what if's of life? The answer is simple; they are just not focused. As time passes life seems become filled with other things and other tasks that slow down our focus. The passion, our dreams, and plans are shifted to worldly matters or what's going on in other people's lives. It is so easy to lose focus. If we are not careful, we will become so busy looking at what we think appears to be greener grass and pastures.

I urge you to think about who you compare yourself to daily. What is stopping you? What is blocking you from reaching to your fullest potential? If you are like me, I always imagined myself being successful. I believed that it was in me to achieve everything I set out to do, however I began to drift. I got way off course because of mere interactions and shifting my energy toward things not of God. Instead I concentrated my efforts on those things I felt would make life seem more enjoyable for me in the form of such things as "relationships."

Have you ever gotten to a place in life when you knew you were closer than ever to your destiny? Like the sweet smell of victory swept by, but then you don't know how to get over the hurdles of bad choices that you have made along your journey of life?

I can be the first to tell you, I completely understand. Sometimes in this thing we call LIFE, we can get stuck. We can take the wrong turn, and even forget to breathe. When I was seven years old I decided to make Jesus my Lord and Savior. I never imagined the events that would proceed afterward. I went through the motions as a child. I said my prayers every night. I went to Sunday and Wednesday church services. I sang in the choir. I even witnessed to my peers. But did I really understand the power in believing God? Did I really see the fruit of my faith?

As I got older, and became a young adult, my life changed. I changed. I saw myself spinning around in circles. I felt like I was on the outside looking in. It was easy to portray the good life. It was easy to put on the big happy Christian smile and act like nothing in the world bothered me. However, I didn't really believe what I preached all the time. I was not always in the shouting mood. As a matter of fact, I cried so much behind closed doors.

It was not until I turned 20 years old that I really began to see the harvest and fruit of the faith I had. Yes, 13 years went by before I really started to understand the power that lied behind simply believing the impossible in life. To the average 21-year-old that would seem like a long time.

God is calling us to believe. Believing is probably the hardest thing to do when everything in your life starts to speak the opposite of what is declared to you. Much of society today is twisted. We have lost our focus. We should be focused on the things of God. Whether we realize it or not, we all have a desire to be in the Will of God in one way or the other. Yet, we search and seek everything but God.

The source of our Hope should not be about what *could* happen with God, but what *will* happen through God. Destiny whispers to us through our daily lives all the time, but what is it that stops us? What is it that causes us to even think about giving up? Some say it is FEAR. Others say it is uncertainty. I say it's the lack of faith.

The very thing the enemy is after is not our material possessions—he is after our minds. That is where we call in the things that we cannot see. Romans 17b says "…and calleth those things which be not as though they were." The Word of God declares in Proverbs 23:7 (KJV) [7] For as he thinketh in his heart, so is he."

What is shifting through our minds? How do we really perceive the life that we are given?

Do not let destiny keep staring you dead in the face without doing anything, but go out there and grab it for what it has to offer for your life. Let your Faith declare your outcome.

Fear is only a negative outlook of what rejection could look like. Time in this life is running out quicker then we can ever imagine. God is calling us to the places and position that he has ordained for us. What the enemy tries to do in your life to stop you will not work! It will not work! Our faith has to go in the fire so that it may come out as pure GOLD. Job 23:10 (KJV) [10] ... when he hath tried me, I shall come forth as gold."

We all are given the power to stand in the midst through faith. I don't care what has happened in your life or what is happening right now. The best for your life is yet to come. I know for a fact that if we lean on Him, that everything will be just fine.

This is the season of transformation and change, but if we don't tap into the anointing and go deeper in God, then we will miss the harvest. The world is crying out for the faith that we have. Believe it or not, the world is waiting on the church to take a stand for God. We, as Christians, cannot be afraid to declare the power of God. It is indeed true that the God that is in us is more than the ones that are against us. Romans 8:31 (KJV) states, "What shall we then say to these things? If God *be* for us, who *can be* against us?"

We are the next generation. It is time to take our streets back, our families back, and our positions back. For too long we have been silent, allowing the enemy to take and say whatever he chooses regarding what belongs to us. In this season, declare that what broke you before will be the thing that will build you up and push you toward your destiny.

Be careful about what you speak over the lives of your children. The children are the seeds to the harvest of restoration upon the earth. Encourage and train the children so they will grow up being the men and women of God that they are supposed to be. It is not the time to remain behind the scenes. Whatever God has placed inside must come out. God does not care if you don't have all the pieces together. All God desire from you is that you be the vessel and He gets the Glory through your test, which is your testimony. It is time to give God your best. Have faith in what you speak. God is saying, "Declare what you need and watch me give you the desires of your heart."

God does not want to be our last resort. He wants to be the first one that we talk to about our dreams, about our plans, and about the desires of our hearts. I promise, if you choose not to include GOD in your plans, you may make what you think are the best plans in the world, but It is only with Him that your steps can properly be ordered and guided in the right way in life. I am not sure where you are in Life right now, But God does not have you reading this book my chance. It is by divine intervention and appointment.

God knows you better than you think he does. Hold on to your Faith. Dare to believe God for what You have not yet seen manifest in your life. I promise you, when you believe God your blessings and breakthroughs are just around the corner.

Life is nothing but a huge faith walks. However, you cannot

allow the bumps to stop you from pursuing your purpose. Take hold of that childlike faith and walk boldly. The battle that you have faced or are facing right now is already won because it belongs to the Kings of Kings and the Lord of Lords. No matter what your age, God still needs you to exercise your gifts for His kingdom. God is in control of your life, and the only person you are to please and give your focus and energy to is Him. Seek God. Believe God. Trust me, believing His Report is always the best choice.

Conclusion

You may be reading this and saying, "I need change. My life is going in the wrong direction and I want to be living anointed in spirit again. I want to able to walk and not faint. I'm weak and I can't handle this burden." I want you to tell God that you are sorry. Stop running from God and say *yes* to His will and *yes* to His way.

You may be reading this and think you have been anointed and appointed by God, but you allowed what people said and did to you to cut off your own blessings. You have let people destroy you mentally and spiritually. Take control and tell God, "I know I let you down God, but I'm truly back now."

You may be reading this while holding a grudge against someone, and it's eating you up every time you see them. Maybe they are going about living their life, but you haven't yet moved on because you buried the pain deep in your heart. It's time to free yourself and let go of all that hurt. It's not worth it. It's not worth the stress you are putting yourself through.

God told me to tell you to keep hope, strength, and faith. It is fine to be laid low for a minute, but once God enters the picture, all worry should be gone. What are you worrying about? Do you not believe in His promises anymore? Those same promises have worked over and over again in the great depths of time. Do you think they have lost their power? If so, I will tell you now that it is surely not the case. God's Word is our sword and we are warriors for Him. No weapon that is formed against us shall succeed—never before and definitely not now. Start over, and this time ask God to enter your heart and direct your path. Do not tune Him out because it is not what you want to hear or because it doesn't fit your lifestyle. You will hurt less and rejoice more!

I encourage you to say to God right now,

"Whatever you are doing in this season, please don't do it without me. God, if you're healing in this season, don't do it without me. God, I need a blessing and miracle and I'm going to stop questioning you and start believing you. God, I'm going to stop holding back my praise because God, you've been too good to me. God, you brought me from a mighty long way. God, I'm trusting in you because I know I'm just a small piece of the puzzle. Thank you for my breakthroughs. God, place my feet on solid ground.

How many chances has God given you? God gives us chances over and over again, but with the second chances you are given, live for Him and not for you. I know the devil has told you that God has forgotten about you. He told you that your situation is hopeless, and he told you that no one loves or cares for you. But

I dare you to look Satan in the face and call him a liar.

Tell Satan to take a walk with you. Begin to declare boldly that he has dragged you along with him for too long and that now you're turning to your savoir and breaking free. Tell Satan, "I am learning to lean and depend on God. My savior died for my sins, loved me so much that he suffered for my mistakes. He carried my burden on his back."

Satan has to know the Savior didn't stay dead, but rose up in all his power and might. Tell him you are the child of the King whose authority you speak on behalf of. That he can't destroy what God has anointed in your life. Tell Satan like you would tell your haters, "You didn't make me and you sure won't break me."

Satan is bold. He wants us to keep backing down in fear and doubt, but we have to stand for God. God knows it gets hard, and He is not expecting perfection, so He allows us to make mistakes. Don't you want to walk in favor through His powerful anointing?

I never imagined how things I felt were so impossible could come to pass, but I realized it was nobody but God in His wisdom. God wants to use you and me for His glory but we have to be able to deny who we are and follow Him wherever He takes us. I am grateful for accepting and thriving on God's place in my life.

I wrote this book because it was a big ministry for my life to begin with. I literally told God and gave Him every excuse to why He could not use me, but after seeing His mighty works, His grace, unconditional love, and most of all the greater transformation that took place in my life, I knew there was no way I could sit down on God's anointing and calling over my life. I just couldn't keep it to myself. I wanted others to know how to, and be able to, experience God's favor, His strength, His Power, and His peace.

God wants us to be so on fire for Him that when He brings us out of darkness, we rejoice. Yet, we keep it to ourselves, never revealing just how good God has been to us. There are going to be people that think you are boasting, but let them know you have come too far to sit down on your God.

Walk in favor, walk in faith, and believe God for who He is. Stop doubting Him and instead praise Him. I dare you to claim victory and not defeat next time you feel you can't go on, and watch my God, your God, and our God fight your battles. Stop trying to figure it out and let God work it out. Stop trying to be God in your own life and let God be God!

Remember, only what we do for Christ will last. Will you be ready? Is God pleased with your life? Is He pleased with the time and effort you give Him? If the answer to any of these questions is *no*, I encourage you to get it right with Him today. May God bless you and forever keep you covered and favored through His blessings.

The Power Behind Faith
Poetry from the Soul

Faith Shaken

I'm trying to keep my faith
So much going on in the world
God how do I keep hope alive
How do I fly
I am running out of time to get it right with you.
Lord, grant me grace
I travel everyday
Thinking about the future and my fate.
Sometimes you can't be traced
Sometimes I don't know what to even say.
God open the door
Shut the past up
Listen to my heart and give me mercy.
I have come so far
Yet my faith is shaken at times
I won't stop at a drop of a dime
No matter how hard it gets in this day and time
I tell myself that everything will be fine.
Trying to hold on to the vision you placed inside
Darkness I have felt, but with you I know light will always shine.
Faith and fear are opposites, right?
So Lord help me overcome the attacks that cause me so many tears.
Fighting through faith.
That's the place I know is truly safe.
In your arms I lay and pray
Seeking your love and warm embrace.
I'm trying to keep my faith
Lord, don't let me go astray.

Give me wisdom and strength to know
That it doesn't matter what the enemy says.
I'm strong, anointed, and mighty
Equipped to run this race.

Called by God

Confused, broken, and disgusted with life
Hide the pain deep inside.
Trying to escape the past,
Buried the pain.
Wake up every day to see the same thing take place
Go to sleep every night with the same old mess.
Praying and pleading for that change
Watching and searching for that miracle.
Just when I thought my life was useless and put to no use
God came and spoke these words to me—
You are not a mistake,
You are not going to inherit those devilish traits
For you are beautiful and wonderfully made, my child.
You are a fighter and a winner
Quitting is the fear of not winning,
And winning is the act of not quitting.
The past you see is over,
The future I hold in my hands,
The heartaches you bear are gone.
Tears turned from sorrow to joy
Joy then turns to peace.
You have a promise to fulfill,
You have so much love in your heart to give,
So why let the devil trick you?
Why let the devil break you down?
I called you to victory
Not despair
Not hurt
Not angry
Not tears.

I called you to a place of peace
A place of strength
I begin to hear Him say.
For you are a witness to my miracles,
A source of my power within.
For I knock day in and day out
For broken, confused souls like yours.
Now do me a favor and let your story
Turn into my glory.
Let your hurt
Let your bruises
Let your broken heart
Touch many minds
Many hearts and many souls.
Then there was silence,
A quick drop to my knees in tears
For I knew my promise, my calling,
And season was due.

The Game of Focus

Destiny is staring you in the face,
I mean can't you taste the sweet victory of success
Your faith is going through fire,
It is going under a series of tests
You started out so strong, bold, and sure
You started out so young
You started out so confident and sure in what you were to do.
Destiny is staring you in the face,
You must refocus your vision and thoughts
You must release the guilt, shame, and doubts.
Maybe you missed the mark
Maybe you turned the wrong corner along the way
But you will not be stopped
You will not give up now
Destiny is staring you in the face.
It is telling you not to let your past
Speak for you anymore.
It is telling you that all things are working for your good
Not one thing was by chance
Now it's time for you to declare freedom in Christ
Time to take a real stance.
Whose report will you believe?
Who will you put your trust in?
Destiny is wiping away the lost time
It's calling you for a divine appointed time.
If you sit back and ponder on what should happened,
Could have happened or would have happened
Destiny will keep staring you in the face
Its time you walk out your faith
For you know the power that lies behind faith.

It is the season to focus on what's ahead
It's the season to step up to the front lines
It's the season to tell God, "Yes" one more time.

I Found the Key

Stuck and planted firmly
On this ground
That is beneath me,
The baggage of life you see
Is getting too heavy for me.
One foot forward,
Yet the others somehow won't move
Caught up in this mess
I feel I must address.
Feel like a bee
That has lost all its honey
The sweet fragrance of life
Is replaced with fight after fight.
Stuck and planted firmly
On this ground
That is beneath me.
The baggage of life you see
Is getting too heavy for me.
Where did all these chains come from?
When did they appear on me?
Was I too much of a Scrooge?
Too selfish and rude?
These chains are getting tighter
I need to break free
But how?
When?
Let go, I tell myself
Relax, because the key is above you
Not beneath.
And this baggage,

Though too heavy for me
Is no match for my King.
One foot forward,
Now I can move the other.
I don't need to address
For this is one of God's tests.
For He is the key
To breaking me free.
Though I couldn't see then,
Now I know
He will never walk out and leave
Me chained and bound
By my own baggage of life.
He came
While I was yet sleeping
To protect me,
To release me from my doubts,
He came so that I can live and shout.
For He is the key
To all the chains in my life
That the devil thought could hold me.
He is the reason I can move both feet again
He gave me my honey back
He is the sweet fragrance of life
So now I know that my chains
Though tight and strange
Can't keep me from my destiny.
For God has showed me
That He is the key
So I can now let go
And break free.

Chosen

Chosen,
A word that can't be explained fully
A word that is to yet to be understood
Chosen.
You were chosen from the beginning
You were hand-picked by God, Himself.
Don't blame your parents
'Cause you were chosen.
If only you knew the power that lies within you.
The boldness that you possess inside.
Chosen
A word that many known but have a hard time receiving
Conceiving the process that it took
The battles to be faced along the way.
The bruises and scars that are hidden behind the call
A dream that speaks loud in troubled times.
Favor that can't be explained
Grace that grabs your life in the times of great storms.
Chosen
A word that defines the strength you were given
The gift that you can't get rid of.
Don't blame the past
It was all a part of the plan
So stand still.
Chosen
Don't let the enemy steal and kill your title,
You are already blessed
Given a promise that no one can steal.
Given a life that many wish they knew.
Chosen

Do you really understand that being chosen is not a game?
It's a lion roaring that can't be tamed.
It's a fight that no one else can defeat but you.
It's an assignment that only you can claim in the midst of your pain.
Yeah, it will be sunshine
But don't forget there will also be much rain.
Don't worry about the drought,
It's only a season to prepare you
It's only a stepping stone for the greater reward that you will get in the end.
Hold your head up.
Hold your hand tight.
Declare that you are powerful
Declare that you have authority.
You will not fail
You will not quit.
Chosen
A word that many love to hear
But many won't ever take on the journey.
Many will claim, yet be detoured
Many will fall off
But you will not let life beat you down
You will grab your integrity
You will walk with purpose
You were chosen by God.
You are His handpicked creation
Don't let fear choke you
Trust me, your life is just beginning
It's nowhere near being through.
Chosen
A word that many run from
Thinking it will lead them in a dark hole
But to be chosen is to say "Yes"

To forget the rest of the story
To walk with faith
Even if that's all that you have
When everything doesn't seem to be going ok.
Chosen
Choose not to run, but rather stay
Knowing there is no time to play
Knowing there is no way to portray,
What you are not, because it will leave a stain of bitterness
But will turn into compassion with tenderness.
Nothing will change
You are chosen
You ride the waves of confidence
You declare peace
And I promise all the mess in your life has to cease.
Believe the impossible
Because destiny lives in your faith.
To be chosen is to know Jesus is always
The reason for each and every season.
Chosen, Yes, you
Know that in spite of judgement
In spite of your other perception
In spite of what you yet understand.
You have been handpicked by the almighty
You have been chosen

Moving Forward

Looking back, but I must move forward
Pain, hurt, anger is all I can feel and see
What happened to me, God?
Where did it all go wrong?
Did I miss a step?
Did I fall too hard this time?
What happened to me, God?
Fighting temptation
Screaming for help, but there was no answer.
Tears after tears
Questions after questions.
I am strong, right? I am a winner, right?
Well, why do I feel like I can't go on?
Why do I feel like my heart is empty?
Yet, my mind is so full.
Can you hear me now, God?
Can you see through my appearance and my smile?
I'm broken
I'm weak
For I have been stripped of my pride, love, and possessions.
Hmmm…Looking back, but I must move forward.
Here I stand with my hands
In praying position
In search for my answer.
What happened to me, God?
Where did it all go wrong?
Did I not love hard enough?
Was I too blind to see
The signs that were planted before me?
On my knees,

Standing by these trees
I've given it all up again.
I'm freeing myself
And giving you my hand.
God help me stand
God, can you hear me now?
There are no distractions
There is nothing but these dreams, it seems.
What happened to me, God?
I am constantly looking back,
But I must move forward, God
One last thing
As I throw away this ring
And cut all strings.
I need to know
The answer to my question.
What do I do now, God?
Sit? Stand? Jump? Skip? Dive?
Confront? Discuss? Seek revenge?
Give in?
Embrace? Or just get facts?
What do I do now, God?
I heard you say,
"Just stay on track
And do not look back.
I'm holding your hand
So just take a stand.
I'm leading your path
In this awful and awkward draft.
Keep the Faith
Keep the Love
Keep the Strength.
My child, my daughter
You are a warrior.

My Word is your sword
Not these fashionable trends.
Just hold on, pray, read,
And don't give in.
Just trust me and begin again.

Know Your Value

Know your value
Look at the people around you.
Yes, they love you
Yes, they need you
You are a power source .
Shout out loud, let the devil
Here the roar of your voice
The clap of your hands
Stomp your feet and repeat
You know you can.
Know your value
Stop letting people define your abilities.
You are not limited by words
Or the eyes of your fellow man.
You are strong and mighty
You are intelligent
You are wise beyond your years.
Quit regretting you experiences
Look at your life
The battles you have faced are over,
Cut down and buried in the sand
They were supposed to stop you
They were assigned to kill you
But, nope they just redirected
And helped to build you.
Look at your hands
Through the sweat and tears
Crawling under the unseen obstacles.
Jumping over the hurdles of your life
Stepping up a latter that you couldn't see.

Know your value
Did you know that you are God's greatest warrior?
I mean, really, who could have survived.
You didn't grow weary and get tired
You refused to stop fighting
Until the victory is what you claimed.
You always found peace as the tornado blew pass your house
When the drought came through
Praise was still on your lips
A few slips here and there
But you made it through.
Did you ever go hungry? No.
Did you ever stop breathing?
No, but I saw you stop believing.
Know your value
You are royalty
You are a vessel that can be
Beaten,
Kicked,
Talked about,
Misunderstood,
Rejected
Overlooked
Yet you won't stop pushing
Preaching the gospel
To the ones who need it most.
Grab your cross
Your soul is not lost
Your spirit is not dead
It just needs to be fed.
Positive thinking this time
Cutting off the dead weight
Dying in the prison is not your fate.
Rise up

With eyes of faith
Stop playing it safe.
You are different
You are formed just the way I planned it.
Full of energy
Full of hope
Stubborn by divine revelation
Desiring to cling to my every word
Praying on the behalf of the saints.
I wish you could see the you
That I see inside and out
What I think about your life
Is the only thing that should count.
Bounce back
Your mistakes were necessary.
They can't delay you any longer
Your blessing is coming
Forming, underneath the dust of depression and loneliness.
You made it
You survived.
Know your value
It's greater than time spinning,
Though I won't pause time
I will stop a sermon for you
I would get a Word through to you
Don't hide
Don't deny
Just obey my voice
Know your value
Bought at a price
With blood that dripped down my son's face
Chest
hands
feet

Just for you
To not give up.
Just for you to pursue
The impossible with no hesitation
With no intimidation.
Know your value
Stop letting people use and abuse you
Sick of seeing you cry avoidable tears.
Life, I set before you
Is only there to increase
To prosper you
Through you I want the glory
No less then what I invested inside you.
Words that need to be spoken
Testimony that's untold
A ministry to be unleashed
A movement to teach.
See through my eyes
Not through your own
Make those connections
Get on that phone.
Only though faith
You will receive
What you need.
Many will want to sow seeds
Many believe in you.
Know your value
Push through the insecurities
You will not go alone
I am there
When all begin to scare.
Look up to me and let me
Speak through thee
I am the root of your tree.

I have the answers you have sought
You are never in need of comfort
I am your warm embrace
Taste the good life.
On the other side of this mountain
Wealth is your fate.
You will have a huge fountain of love
That flows from your heart.
Children will gravitate to you
They will look up to you
Wondering where to go and what to do.
I am sending out the angels
Your souls can't wait any longer
Stop sitting, pondering,
It is time.
Know your Value
The anointing
The passion
The power
The prayer
The plan
It is all coming together.
Hold on to my word
Prepare for the best time of your life.
Know your value
Let me take control
Let me show you why you were created so bold.
Let me write the story that was never told.

The Laborers are Few

The laborers are few
You asked for the impossible
You prayed for the blessing
You sought the answers
But when will you put forth my work?
When will you study my word?
Declare the truth behind the lies
Proclaim that I am the only one
Proclaim that Hell is real and judgement will surely come!
You are to stand for what is right
Fighting the good fight till the end
You have no choice
There is no debate on the call I placed on your life.
You can fight it
You can deny it
Yet you will never get rid of it
It will follow you to the clubs
It will follow you to the casino
It will present itself strong anytime trouble is near.
Killing your flesh and making your spirit stronger
Dying everyday
Shaping your character and maturing your mind.
You are to be a warrior
You are to bc wiser
You have no reason to doubt me.
You have seen me on the mountaintop
You have seen me in the trends
You have walked through the wilderness with me.
Blind to the clear vision
Struggling to see what I see.

Struggling to break the barriers
You will not back down anymore
You will rise to the occasion
You will reach the place of victory.
The laborers are few
They have no clue
How hard the journey is when you fight against God's purpose.
His will
His direction
When will we as His Chosen people wake up?
When will we see that complacency is not the key!
We are not to get comfortable
We are not to look for the storms to cease!
We are just to believe God.
The laborers are few
We want peace but war is what we start in ourselves.
Trying to serve two masters
Being one person here and another
Somewhere else.
The work of God is not a game
It is an assignment
It is an honor.
Grab your cross
Bury the hurt and forgive
It's time to walk into your harvest
It's time you rest and live.
Live for your God.
Serve your God.
Defend your God
You know He is real.
Live the Life that is preached
They will come
They will seek
They will convert you

Just don't stop believing.
Hold on to what you know
Hold on to what you have seen with your own eyes.
Do not let go just yet
Wrestle with God
Plead with God
Pray and Worship God.
He is with you.
He knows you.
He has heard you.
Wake up
The laborers are few
That's why God has called you.
Yes, He really needs you.
Every gift
Every word
Every book
Every testimony.
Stop holding back
The manifestation is near.
Get back on that boat.
Don't drown in your tears
The storm is ceasing
The waves are slowing down.
Here comes your rescue
The shore is near!

Keeping Faith

I'm trying to keep my faith
So much going on in the world
God, how do I keep hope alive
How do I fly?
I am running out of time to get it right with you.
Lord, grant me grace
I travel everyday
Thinking about the future and my fate.
Sometimes you can't be traced
Sometimes I don't know what to even say.
God, open the door
Shut the past up
Listen to my heart and give me mercy.
I have come so far
Yet, my faith is shaken at times.
I want stop at a drop of a dime
No matter how hard it gives in this day and time
I tell myself that everything will be fine.
Trying to hold on to the vision you placed in me
Darkness I have felt
But with you I know light will always shine.
Faith and fear are opposites, right?
So, Lord, help me overcome the attacks that cause me so many
tears.
Fighting through faith.
That's the place I know is truly safe.
In your arms I lay and pray
Seeking your love and warm embrace.
I'm trying to keep my faith
Lord, don't let me go astray.

Give me wisdom and strength to know
That it doesn't matter what the enemy says.
I'm strong, anointed, and mighty
Equipped to run this race.

Claim It

Stand on my word
Fight with your sword
Live in the truth. You are a winner
You back down from no fight
Release the giant in you.
Walk into your destiny
With expectation
With victory.
The hardest part you climbed over
The mountain is moving by faith
The valley is disappearing through grace
Joy is peaking from within
Tears will stop following.
You will see the you
You were born to be
The you that you were destined and created to be
I am turning it all around
I am shifting the direction in your life
Stand firm, hold down your fort
Break down the walls
Of doubt
Grief
Regret
Negativity
Guilt.
Don't worry about your enemies
Don't look back to see what's behind

Move forward
Pursue the next level
Draw from your heart
Knowledge is power
Activate your supernatural power
Dig deep down
Keep seeking
Keep asking
Keep writing
Keep speaking.
No way
Can you throw in the towel now
No way
Can you let go now.
You are too close
You are too anointed
Called
Chosen
Proven
Tested
Trained.
Your inheritance
Is Huge
Say it
Name it
Declare it
Claim it.

Stand Still

Stand still
Hold on
Don't stress yourself out.
Stand still
I am always in control
I am always working behind the scenes.
Stand still
Fight the good fight of faith
Pray for your enemies
You can't figure it all out
I am ending your drought.
Stand still
Search from within
Focus on Jesus
The author
The string to purpose
The Name above all others.
Stand still
Don't yield to the temptation
Don't get lost in the temporary attacks.
Stand still
Yes…You
I am your ultimate supply
I am all you will ever need
You cannot see the blessings
But they are all around
You were born blessed.
Stand still
I got you
I want you

I chose you
I ordained you
I requalified you
I protected you.
I empowered you
Shifted you
Sought for you
Found you.
Stand still
Nothing has changed
The enemy has not won.
Stand still
Let me impart
Let me give
You a spiritual refill
Now that you are healed
I can start the rebuild process.
Stand still
Do not rebuke
Do not let people get in your head.
My plan
Is to give you
Your expected end.

About Tameka Hicks

Tameka Hicks can be described as a passionate, persistent, dedicated, and God-fearing lady, author, and poet. She discovered her purpose and God's will for her life at age 18. She quoted, "Life is not a game, but there is a playing field and we must all choose our coach." She understands the dangers of trying to serve two masters. She constantly lives by one of her most known inspirations, Maya Angelou's quote, "We may encounter many defeats but we must not be defeated." She has faced much pain, heartache, and many battles in her life but refuses to be defeated. She aspires to speak her story all over the nation to hurting men and women to help them understand that if she made it through, they can and will too.

Ms. Hicks is not only a writer but desires to be a CEO of a fortune 500 company and build her own ministry. She has a real passion for writing and speaking the Word of God, and everywhere she goes she wears a smile.

Tameka was born in Memphis, Tennessee on June 1, 1994. At three years old she was adopted to a single mother, Brenda Hicks, and was raised in Jackson, Tennessee. She also has loving godparents, Geraldine King-Fields and Stanley Fields. She is an outgoing person, and has a humbling spirit. No matter where she goes, she acknowledges that God is first in her life, and that she is nothing without Him.

She has been known to inspire, motivate, and transform many lives through the anointing of God and the testimony of her personal battles. She loves to dance, sing, and enjoy her time with her family and friends. She strongly believes that if she can save one soul or inspire one person, then her story is truly worth telling. She plans to serve and walk in God's will for the rest of her life.

You can contact Tameka Hicks via the following social media sources

https://www.linkedin.com/in/tameka-hicks-0a057467/
https://m.facebook.com/tameka.hicks
YouTube - Tameka Hicks
Instagram- Tlhicks23
Website: http://tamekahicks460.wixsite.com/saidiwouldnttell

Editorial Reviews
http://www.theusreview.com/reviews/Said-Hicks.html#.WoDq4nBMGEc
https://www.eastcountymagazine.org/said-i-wouldnt-tell-itbut-i-just-cant-keep-it-myself